T0382653

Dynamic Growth of Chinese Firms in the Global Market

How have Chinese multinationals benefitted from China's economic boom to enable their international expansion? This book is based on many years of original research tracing the emergence, growth, and future of Chinese firms in the world economy. The authors seek to provide new perspectives and insights for business executives and graduate students through a comprehensive study of how China's firms globalise, operate, and the implications of this for economic success. Based on detailed case studies and summative examples of *successful* Chinese firms, Tse and Hung point out their strengths (e.g., making innovations affordable to many developing nations), their weaknesses (e.g., products made in China are not highly regarded), and their mistakes (e.g., being insensitive to host economy needs and at times corruptive acts). They argue that the world economy would benefit from engaging with Chinese and other emerging economy firms to learn from the strategies they employ to achieve their global reach.

DAVID K. TSE is Stelux Professor and Chair Professor of International Marketing and Director of the Contemporary Marketing Centre at the University of Hong Kong. He is a world-class scholar in international marketing, marketing in China and international business. He also consults for a wide range of companies in China, Hong Kong and Canada.

KINETA HUNG is Professor at the Hong Kong Baptist University. Her works have appeared in the Journal of Marketing, the Journal of International Business Studies and the Journal of Advertising among others. Rated as a world's leading advertising scholar, she serves on the Editorial Board of the Journal of Advertising and the American Academy of Advertising Research Council and has given academic and executive talks in Hong Kong, China and overseas.

Dynamic Growth of Chinese Firms in the Global Market

Challenges, Strategies, and Implications

DAVID K. TSE
University of Hong Kong

KINETA HUNG
Hong Kong Baptist University

CAMBRIDGE
UNIVERSITY PRESS

University Printing House, Cambridge CB2 8BS, United Kingdom

One Liberty Plaza, 20th Floor, New York, NY 10006, USA

477 Williamstown Road, Port Melbourne, VIC 3207, Australia

314–321, 3rd Floor, Plot 3, Splendor Forum, Jasola District Centre,
New Delhi – 110025, India

79 Anson Road, #06–04/06, Singapore 079906

Cambridge University Press is part of the University of Cambridge.

It furthers the University's mission by disseminating knowledge in the pursuit of
education, learning, and research at the highest international levels of excellence.

www.cambridge.org
Information on this title: www.cambridge.org/9781107060128
DOI: 10.1017/9781107446731

© David K. Tse and Kineta Hung 2020

First published 2020

Printed in the United Kingdom by TJ International Ltd. Padstow Cornwall

A catalogue record for this publication is available from the British Library.

Library of Congress Cataloging-in-Publication Data
Names: Tse, David Kwai-Che, author. | Hung, Kineta, author.
Title: Dynamic growth of Chinese firms in the global market : challenges,
strategies and implications / David K. Tse, University of Hong Kong,
Kineta Hung, Hong Kong Baptist University.
Description: Cambridge, United Kingdom ; New York, NY : Cambridge
University Press, 2020. | Includes bibliographical references and index.
Identifiers: LCCN 2019038386 (print) | LCCN 2019038387 (ebook) | ISBN
9781107060128 (hardback) | ISBN 9781107446731 (epub)
Subjects: LCSH: Corporations – China. | International business enterprises – China.
| China – Commerce.
Classification: LCC HD2910 .T84 2020 (print) | LCC HD2910 (ebook) |
DDC 338.8/8951–dc23
LC record available at https://lccn.loc.gov/2019038386
LC ebook record available at https://lccn.loc.gov/2019038387

ISBN 978-1-107-06012-8 Hardback
ISBN 978-1-107-62975-2 Paperback

Contents

Figures

Tables

1 Introduction

1.1 CHINA'S ECONOMIC REFORM AND GROWTH: THE AWAKENING OF THE SLEEPING DRAGON

From Haier to Lenovo, and from Huawei to Alibaba, Chinese firms are going outside the country looking for resources, technology, markets, and a major global presence. This is a relatively new phenomenon in the world's economy, as practically all modern Chinese corporations were founded no more than thirty years ago, after the opening up and subsequent marketisation of the Chinese economy in the early 1980s. In 1979, when China only produced 2.6 per cent of the global GDP, no one could have forecasted that China would become the world's second largest economy, whose firms can compete with, and at times outcompete, renowned and established corporate giants in some of the most competitive industries.

Indeed, marked by its bold, unique, and dynamic economic policies, China's economic growth is unmatched in economic history. At the time of its awakening, the country focused on developing an export-led manufacturing base to take advantage of the country's large pool of low-cost factory workers. Between 1980 and 1984, its four special economic zones were set up in Shenzhen, Zhuhai, Shantou, and Xiamen, with special economic policies, tax incentives, and reduced regulations aimed at attracting foreign investments and technology. Another fourteen coastal cities joined the scheme in 1984, following the success of the new policy on the economic zones, and, by the late 1980s, similar policies were made in eighty-four of its coastal cities. While the policy initially attracted factory owners originating from Hong Kong and Chinese Taiwan, these special economic zones became highly attractive to established multinational corporations (MNCs) from different countries. They invested in these zones to take advantage of the low production costs, favourable policies, and the business ecosystems with their concentration of suppliers, logistics, and services that serve the manufacturing hubs (Bajpai, 2014). Some MNCs subsequently shifted a proportion of their manufacturing function to China, making the country the 'world factory' in many labour-intensive industries.

The economic activities undertaken in the special economic zones not only provided benefits to these regions, but also 'radiated' to other parts of the country and sped up China's economic growth. Among them was the transformation of China's state-owned enterprises (SOEs), which were known to be notoriously inefficient prior to the 1980s. Haier, a consumer electronics and home appliance giant, was a typical example of SOEs of the time, with its dilapidated infrastructure, poor management, outdated technology, and lack of financial resources. Nevertheless, after Zhang Ruimin took the helm in 1984, the company reinvented itself four times over the next twenty years to succeed in the global environment of today (Fischer, Lago, and Liu, 2015). According to BusinessWire (2015), Haier now has the largest market share worldwide in white goods (i.e., domestic appliances). Other SOEs such as those in resource-based industries (e.g., SINOPEC, State Grid) have also completely transformed their business models over the past thirty years to compete in the world market.

While many of China's SOEs have transformed into global players, China's private firms also flourished, driven by and taking advantage of the country's economic momentum, its vibrant business ecosystems, and the strong and robustly growing market demand over the past decades. As SOEs retreated from their inefficient multibusiness orientation to focus on their core business in order to improve their economic efficiency, non-core business opportunities emerged for small and medium-sized private enterprises (SMEs) to advance in these and other formerly restricted industries. Some privately owned enterprises (POEs) took over labour-intensive industries in textiles, rubber, medicines, general machinery, and printing that once were the domains of SOEs. Others took advantage of the business ecosystems that evolved in nonmanufacturing sectors. Some, surprisingly, even went after the high-technology industries.

The exemplary case of the last approach can be found in Shenzhen, a once idle and economically marginalised region north of Hong Kong that has now become the Silicon Valley of China. Shenzhen is home to Tencent, Huawei, BGI (genome research institute), BYD (automobiles and new energy), and ZTE (telecom) (He, 2015), and it boasts one of the highest concentrations of technology start-ups in China (Bloomberg News, 2016). According to the China Statistical Yearbook (2012), more than 60 per cent of the country's research-and-development (R&D) spending and, since 2012, 65 per cent of the country's patent applications came from POEs, making the private sector a highly contestable contributor to the Chinese economy as well as a strong player in the world market. Indeed, POEs such as Alibaba, Tencent, Huawei, Sina, and Baidu are vibrant players in the highly competitive IT sector, with Huawei making Interband's 2018 list of the best global brands.

I.2   GLOBALISATION OF CHINESE FIRMS

The rise of Chinese firms and their global footprints represent a new and salient phenomenon in international business and the global economy. Building on their manufacturing bases, many Chinese firms climbed up the value chain to become brand and patent holders taking advantage of the global market. As described in an article in Businessweek (Mahajan, 2014), while Lenovo sold only PCs and only in China ten years ago, 'Now it sells PCs, phones, tablets and servers in more than 160 countries'. Other firms, such as the auto-glass manufacturer Fuyao Group, are moving their factories outside of China in search of lower costs and better incentives, as China's wages have soared over the past decade (Mui, 2016). Whereas the rationale for going global may differ, Chinese firms are becoming MNCs in their own right, seeking the best opportunities globally to advance themselves.

This globalisation trend will likely continue as Chinese firms evolve and become more confident global players. A newly released report from the Boston Consulting Group (2018) listed the top 100 up-and-coming firms in the world. Among them were twenty-eight Chinese companies across various industries, including Alibaba Group Holding Limited, Citic Group, Dalian Wanda Group Company, Xiaomi Corporation, and China Eastern Airlines Corporation. The successful firms in China are outperforming their competitors; they are also increasingly buying foreign firms and expanding into new markets that provide them with opportunities not available within China (Zhu and Zhu, 2016). In sum, the trend towards globalisation among Chinese firms is a sustainable phenomenon, and its impact will be felt in the years to come.

As the 'going out' of Chinese firms becomes a sustainable phenomenon, it raises some interesting questions: What are the drivers and business models that allow these firms to grow and succeed in a relatively short time? Did they follow the classical globalisation models (e.g., Dunning seminal model) based on the experiences of MNCs in developed economies, or did they evolve new models based on the contexts in which they operate? Would these alternative models be relevant to firms based in other emerging economies? Of special interest are SOEs, as many globalising Chinese firms are state owned. Given their state ownership, SOEs often become a source of friction between China and its trading partners. Yet, what are the roles SOEs play in the Chinese economy, and how are they organised? How would the SOEs' experiences revive discussion regarding the advantages and pitfalls of state capitalism?

The globalisation of firms in China coincides with similar development of firms in other emerging economies. Firms such as India's IT giant Infosys, South Korea's LG Electronics, Mexico's global leader in building materials Cemex, and Brazil's world-leading producer of iron ore Vale, to name a few, are fuelling the next wave of economic growth as they seize shares in the global market. An interesting question is: What are the factors that enable and drive these firms to grow and prosper when they lack the country advantages enjoyed by MNCs from developed economies?

Researchers have only recently begun to recognise the contributions of emerging-market MNCs as game changers in international business. Despite their lack of country advantages, these firms are devising new globalisation models and leveraging characteristics of the digital economy to drive their growth and build global businesses (Chattopadhyay, Batra, and Ozsomer, 2012). This book investigates MNCs in China with the goal of contributing to this effort to understand emerging-market MNCs, as these firms strike a globalisation path relevant to the context that gives rise to their growth.

1.3 ORGANISATION OF THE BOOK

This book is organised into four parts. The first part examines the salience and implications of globalising Chinese firms. There are two chapters. Chapter 1 provides an overview of this new yet salient phenomenon, while Chapter 2 traces Chinese firms' global footprints, including their momentum and directions. Both SOEs and POEs will be examined.

The second part contains the core section of the book, exploring the different models of firm globalisation and their exemplary cases. It begins by laying out in Chapter 3 the classic globalisation model, whereby firms extend globally to take advantage of the competitive edge they have gained from operating in their home country. While it is the classical model that represents the basic approach to globalisation and has been used successfully by MNCs originated from developed economies, it may not be as applicable to firms originating from emerging economies. It is in this context that we propose, in Chapters 3 and 4, three alternative models undertaken by Chinese firms: the national developmental need model, the springboard model, and the mixed model. Rather than leveraging the competitive advantages built up from their home-country operations, these Chinese MNCs take their lack of competitive advantages as an incentive to reach out globally for resources, technology/expertise, or a global brand name that they cannot source within the home country. These models are used primarily by resource firms/SOEs, banks, and POEs. Chapters 3 and 4 outline and describe each model and then illustrate it using detailed case studies of firms that have either pioneered the model or applied it in their globalisation efforts. The firms examined include Haier, Chalco (national developmental need model), China Merchants Bank (CMB) (springboard model), and Huawei (mixed model). These alternative models represent a paradigm shift in international business.

The third part is another key section of the book. Whereas the second part takes a macro view of globalisation models, the third part takes a micro view and examines the specific failures and challenges faced by globalising Chinese firms. Some of them are faced with difficulties setting up niche markets, while others have difficulties executing mergers and acquisitions. As China is an emerging economy, the challenges faced by Chinese MNCs are new, and the approaches to overcome these hurdles are highly unique. Chapter 5 reports comprehensive cases of TCL, Lenovo, and Citic Pacific Mining to illustrate the challenges these MNCs face and the steps they take to overcome these challenges. Meanwhile, practically all of these firms are faced with, at different degrees, the challenges imposed by an unfavourable country image. The label 'made in China' carries with it negative connotations such as low wages, poor working conditions, low quality, and unsafe products that affect not only consumer attitude, but also consumers' purchase decisions. These negative stereotypes are especially ingrained in the minds of consumers in developed countries. In addition to resolving production problems, Chinese MNCs need to identify the consumer segments in developed countries that are most open and receptive to firms and products from China (Chapter 6).

There are many accounts of MNCs undertaking corporate social responsibility (CSR) activities to attempt to build a relationship with and engage locals in the host country. Most of the accounts in international business concern developed-economy MNCs working in emerging-economy host countries. The issues faced by Chinese MNCs are as follows: How would host market consumers view an emerging economy MNC, and what types of CSR would be appropriate to undertake? Should they undertake CSR activities similar to developed market MNCs? Should they differentiate between developed economy and emerging economy host countries? As data from Chapter 7 show, while CSR activities may help improve the image of Chinese MNCs in the eyes of developed-economy consumers, the first priority should be product safety, which exerts a more significant effect. Chapter 8 wraps up the issue of managing national image by tracing China's image in the international community over the past decade and the issues that affect positive or negative worldviews on China. In addition, the chapter traces the effects of two campaigns initiated by China to attempt to improve its image among major trading partners.

As one would expect, Chinese firms have their fair share of globalisation challenges and failures. Thus, these chapters discuss the weak spots of the Chinese firms. They centre on several types of challenges they face and how some of them have failed. Their weak spots include inexperienced global management, lack of high-value-added capabilities, and lack of knowledge in managing overseas country issues. In addition, the international community has exerted fair and equitable demands for Chinese firms to be good global corporate citizens. Given the economic power of these Chinese firms, failure to meet these standards is increasingly questioned by the host country and the global community. These chapters also discuss how the Chinese firms are addressing these issues at both the country government level and the corporate level.

The fourth part, including Chapters 9 and 10, offers a summative view of the foregoing issues and their future impacts on the globalising firms. Chapter 9 discuss the three aspects that China's government has set up, including a large pool of tech talents, trade relationships with other nations and the Belt-and-Road initiative (BRI). These three aspects exert salient impacts for the Chinese firms. Chapter 10 assumes a summative and futuristic view of the issues discussed in the book. It discusses the challenges that the globalising Chinese firms offer to the world economy as well as the impacts that the world economy exerts on the Chinese firms. The chapter ends with implications for other emerging economies and firms from these economies. If, indeed, the globalisation of Chinese firms is an unprecedented phenomenon in corporate history, it would be highly valuable to ascertain what new business models can be learned from it.

1.4 TARGET AUDIENCE

The book is targeted at three major groups of readers: managers, management (MBA) students, and policymakers. Among managers, it is useful to those who already have some basic knowledge of China, its economy and its firms, as well as managers interested in working with Chinese firms. The book presents useful and relevant overarching frameworks for readers to understand and extrapolate insights from the contextual facts and exemplary company practices. Accordingly, the contents may help deepen the readers' understanding of how Chinese firms in selected sectors develop and grow to become global players using alternative models, as well as, when applicable, how these firms provide benefits to consumers in host countries.

To managers working in firms originating from other emerging economies, such as Brazil, India, Russia, South Africa, and some other Asian countries, the success of Chinese firms' globalisation as outlined in this book provides much-needed encouragement and insights. By understanding the humble beginning of many successful Chinese firms and their refusal to accept global industry norms, firms in other emerging economies may obtain a glimpse of their corporate future and boost their confidence in their globalisation efforts. The overarching frameworks and exemplary company practices outlined in this book also provide, to a lesser extent, models of globalisation for these managers to emulate and reflect upon. However, while some of the Chinese firms' practices can offer insights, we hasten to point out that their successes are unique and may not be repeatable in other contexts in a rapidly changing global landscape.

The book also provides insights to policymakers, both from China and from other countries. Recognising that the globalisation of Chinese firms will persist and that the development over the past ten years is a mere prelude of the firms' momentum, policymakers need to develop a full understanding of the workings of these firms, as well as their behaviours and aspirations. Regarding policymakers in China, they may need to devise guidelines to ensure that outgoing Chinese firms behave properly in host economies and markets to address issues brought about by the presence of Chinese firms that are pertinent to the host countries and cannot be relieved by CSR efforts alone. The policies or guidelines may include alignment with global standards to deter corruption and product hazards and to ensure food safety, as well as good employee practices and local community engagement. These devices are essential for the long-term viability of Chinese firms, their globalisation efforts, and host market acceptance.

For host-country policymakers, the challenges in integrating Chinese firms into the local community and business ecosystem need to be balanced with the benefits these firms may bring to the host country. As noted in the various company cases in this book, many of the global Chinese firms are inexperienced in the global arena. Nevertheless, they are highly flexible as they learn about the workings of the host countries. Thus, the best way forward for both parties may lie in co-developing meaningful and effective policies to channel the entrepreneurial energy that Chinese firms have and translate it into benefits for consumers and employees in the host country. Compared to established global corporations, young Chinese firms may be more accommodating and more willing to work with host-country policymakers, accepting these adjustments as part of their learning curve. We posit that an in-depth knowledge of these corporations may help define a co-development path that is mutually beneficial. This path is especially salient for emerging and developing economy host countries into which many Chinese firms are expanding.

1.5 SPECIAL FEATURES OF THE BOOK

Chinese firms are complex and game-changing organisations in the global economy. Driven by their sociocultural predispositions, they are unique in many ways. Here, we outline three essential elements that characterise these firms. First, it is important to recognise that leading Chinese firms that have gone global have broken established protocols in firm globalisation approaches. Amid the harsh reality where many of the industries in which these firms venture were already filled with powerful, established MNCs, the Chinese firms' success in establishing global footprints has rewritten industry standards and redrawn global market structures in certain industries. The achievements of these leading Chinese firms are remarkable.

Second, in spite of their enviable achievements, these firms are young and are learning organisations. These characteristics allow them to readily adapt to the new digital economy. While being young has advantages, including being less rigid and highly entrepreneurial, it also has the disadvantages of growing pains and many blind spots. Externally, these firms have limited international experiences. This is especially pertinent when they deal with host governments and other stakeholders, whose expectations of firm behaviour may diverge substantially from the expectations of stakeholders in the home market. Internally, many of these firms have yet to acquire global standard practices to allow the headquarters to govern properly the actions and behaviour of their international branches and subsidiaries. It is therefore inevitable that their international operations make 'naive' and clumsy mistakes.

Third, up to this point, Chinese firms' desire for global expansion is driven more by their ego than their economic needs. Except for smaller, specialised Chinese firms that have identified the overseas market as the key provider of their future growth, many Chinese firms remain focused on the domestic market. Rather than venturing strongly into the global arena, these firms use their global presence more as a tactic to improve their stature and appeal in the home market as established MNCs than as a strategy that fully integrates domestic and international operations. Indeed, few of the outgoing Chinese firms earn significant shares of their revenue from their overseas operations; instead, they use their home market demands to support their host market positions. This is especially true of the SOEs. Thus, Chinese firms' mindset and strategy need to be more adaptive and flexible to become truly global. In addition, their structures and processes need to be further developed to support a truly global operation. As the firms' global ventures grow, they may gradually develop the vision, management processes, operating systems, and governance structures that are commensurate with their stature as MNCs.

Given these unique characteristics of outgoing Chinese firms, we as academics intend to share our years of research and insights in Chinese firms with readers of this book. **We have chosen three distinct ways to organise our thoughts**, as described here.

First, we structure the book with an intellectual mindset. Rather than delivering the contents as journalistic reports, we anchor our discussion within overarching frameworks, allowing readers to integrate the decades of change in China and in specific industries to appreciate their impacts on firm strategies and their global footprints. Second, we trace the historical foundation of a topic in each chapter, unfold the relevant layers of institutions (including government influences, sociocultural forces, and personal values), and discuss insights into the management structures and organisational dimensions of selected firms. Third, to provide stronger investigation and empirical support, we report in this book some of our original empirical research and its findings. These studies and findings can be found in Chapters 6, 7, and 8.

As teachers in executive courses and seminars, we understand the value of in-depth case studies in unfolding the complex dimensions involved in management decisions. This book reports in-depth case studies in Chapters 3, 4, and 5 to illustrate the contexts that give rise to the issues faced by Chinese MNCs and the way forwards for these firms to resolve the problems by devising and using various globalisation models. There are a total of six comprehensive case studies: Haier, Lenovo, Chalco, Citic, Huawei, and TCL. These case analyses report the best practices and the implications for firms in their respective industries.

In sum, the book provides intellectual insights into the institu-tional framework in China and, in particular, the home-based advan-tages offered by the country as well as the disadvantages brought about by the poor national image that most Chinese firms have to confront and manage. The book also examines the organisational structures and processes of successful outgoing Chinese firms. Their abilities to learn and their entrepreneurial spirit are especially important for the achieve-ment of these young, inexperienced firms venturing into the interna-tional arena. Finally, the book examines historical changes in China and their impacts on firms by tracing these events through easy to understand time-lines. We hope that the **three ways we used to organise our discussion** in this book will allow readers to penetrate the workings of Chinese firms going global and arrive at a deeper understanding of their impacts, best practices, and future implications.

REFERENCES

Bajpai, P. (2014). Why China Is 'The World's Factory'. *Investopedia.* 22 October. Retrieved 10 January 2019. www.investopedia.com/articles/investing/102214/ why-china-worlds-factory.asp.

Bloomberg News. (2016). China's Factory to the World Is in a Race to Survive. *Bloomberg News.* 6 June. Retrieved 10 January 2019. www.bloomberg.com/news/ articles/2016-06-05/china-s-factory-to-the-world-is-in-a-race-to-survive.

Boston Consulting Group. (2018). The Most Innovative Companies 2018. 17 January. Retrieved 10 January 2019. www.bcg.com/publications/collec tions/most-innovative-companies-2018.aspx.

BusinessWire (2015). Haier Sustains Pole Position in the Euromonitor Global Major Appliances' 2014 Brands Rankings for the Sixth Consecutive Year. BusinessWire

9 January. Retrieved 10 January 2019. https://businesswireindia.com/news/news-details/haier-sustains-pole-position-euromonitor-global-major-appliances-2014-brands-rankings-sixth-consecutive-year/42157.

Chattopadhyay, A., Batra, R., and Ozsomer, A. (2012). *The New Emerging Market Multinationals: Four Strategies for Disrupting Markets and Building Brands*. New York: McGraw-Hill.

China Statistical Yearbook. (2012). Retrieved 2 July 2019. www.stats.gov.cn/tjsj/ndsj/2012/indexeh.htm.

Fischer, B., Lago, U., and Liu, F. (2015). The Haier Road to Growth. *Strategy +Business*. 27 April. Retrieved 2 July 2019. www.strategy-business.com/article/00323?gko=c8c2a.

He, H. (2015). Top 5 Tech Giants Who Shape Shenzhen, 'China's Silicon Valley'. *South China Morning Post.* 17 April. Retrieved 10 January 2019. www.scmp.com/lifestyle/technology/enterprises/article/1765430/top-5-tech-giants-who-shape-shenzhen-chinas-silicon.

Mahajan, N. (2014). Understanding the Globalization of Chinese Companies. CKGSB Knowledge. 30 July. Retrieved 23 July 2019. http://knowledge.ckgsb.edu.cn/2014/07/30/china-business-strategy/understanding-the-globalization-of-chinese-companies/.

Mui, Y. Q. (2016). A Chinese Billionaire Is Staking His Legacy – and Thousands of American Jobs – on This factory in Ohio. *Washington Post.* 26 October. Retrieved 2 July 2019. www.washingtonpost.com/news/wonk/wp/2016/10/26/a-chinese-billionaire-is-staking-his-legacy-and-thousands-of-american-jobs-on-this-factory-in-ohio/?utm_term=.a6d781724544.

Zhu, H. and Zhu, Q. (2016). Mergers and acquisitions by Chinese firms: a review and comparison with other mergers and acquisitions research in the leading journals. *Asia Pacific Journal of Management*, 33(4): 1107–49.

2   China's Economic Rise and Global Footprints of Chinese Firms

2.1   INTRODUCTION

This chapter explores the footprints, drivers, and patterns of Chinese firms in the global economy. It begins by tracing several milestones of the Chinese economy and its firms, including China's initial rise to economic power and its continuous waves of economic transformation. As such, the chapter provides a causal context for us to understand the characteristics and the momentum of globalising Chinese firms and their implications. In addition to laying out the globalisation patterns of Chinese firms, the chapter also discusses the challenges these firms face in the different foreign markets in which they operate.

2.2   CHINA'S ECONOMIC RISE

2.2.1   *The Start of China's Economic Power (1979)*

In 1979, while the rest of the world saw no major events, China's economy woke up. This was the turning point after a long fall that began in 1820, when China contributed 33 per cent of the world's GDP (Figure 2.1). A series of wars (civil wars in China's Qing dynasty and World War II) and technological advances in the developed nations had decimated China's comparative economic strength. By 1979, China contributed only 2 per cent to the world's GDP. At USD182 GDP per capita, and housing more than 20 per cent of the global population, China was ranked among the world's poorest nations.

The country was highly vulnerable economically, because any natural disaster would likely lead to large-scale famine and starvation. In addition to the series of wars it had faced, several significant events

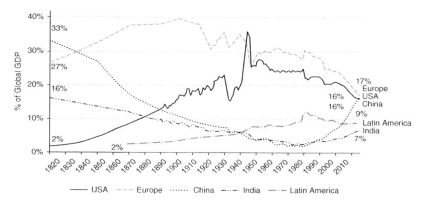

FIGURE 2.1 Percentage of global GDP of selected countries, 1820–2014
Source: United Nations (2018)

had contributed to China's weak economy. For example, in 1962, China's economy was severely damaged as the country cut its previously strong alliance with the Soviet Union. Without the Soviet Union's technological support, China fell far behind the developed world's advancement and devolved into a poor, inefficient, and agricultural-based nation. Further, a poor attempt at economic planning (Great Leap Forward: 1958–61) that led to the destructive Cultural Revolution (1960–7) devastated much of China's economic system and infrastructure.

Thus, in the wake of China's economic transformation in 1979, China was far behind other countries in terms of economic development, infrastructure, and production technology. At that time, there was hardly any seed of economic growth in this populous nation, and no one would have expected China to become a world economic power in any foreseeable future.

In 1979, China had no privately owned enterprises; its SOEs were the only institutions that the nation possessed to produce and feed its mass population. The SOEs followed 'orders' given by the state-planned system that specified the factories' and farms' output quotas to meet the country's needs. In addition to their production roles, the SOEs were also responsible for fulfilling their workers' economic and social needs, including schooling, healthcare, housing, and retirement benefits. The SOEs were designed to be self-contained and self-sufficient units that looked after their workers from birth to death (Qian, 2000).

In this planned regime, the workers were motivated by communist ideals. In all farms, offices, and factories, all workers had more or less the same pay irrespective of ranks. There were no financial rewards to encourage them to work harder or improve the quality of their output. The 'spiritual ideal' was the sole source of all motivation. Externally, China's economy was disconnected from the rest of the world, except for international trades with 'comrade-brother' nations including Cuba, Yugoslavia, and Pakistan (Deng, 2014).

2.2.2 The Turning Point in China's Economy

Initiated by its visionary leader Deng Xiaoping, China has embarked on a series of continuous, overlapping, and multisphere reforms from 1979 to the present day. The country has chosen a planned, stage-wise reform path for its complex economy and society (Nolan, 2001), in contrast to the 'big-bang' reform paths adopted by the former Soviet Union states. As shown in Table 2.1, reforms in China have not stopped for the last forty years.

2.2.3 From Planned Economy to Marketisation and Privatisation

China's earliest reform emphasised marketisation; that is, it allowed the price and supply of products to follow market demand (Lau, Tse, and Zhou, 2002). This reform eased price controls and abolished output quotas in many of China's factories. At the same time, private firms were permitted to be established, and for the first time since 1949, the seed of private ownership was sown. It would take another fifteen years before private property rights (i.e., the rights of people and firms to legitimately own property) were recognised as part of China's constitution in 2004.

Table 2.1 *Summary outline of China's reform, 1978–present*

Timeline	Nature of reform	Specific developments
1978–92	Marketisation	Township and village enterprises
		Dual price system
		Household responsibility system
		Legal status of private business
		Special economic zones
1993–2001	Firm reform	SOE reform
		Budget reform
		Banking restructuring
		Unified exchange rate
		Private housing market
		World Trade Organisation entry
2002–present	Globalisation	RMB re-evaluation
		Offshore RMB market
		Internet rate liberalisation

During this first stage of reform (1978–92), there were continuous ideological debates at the national level. To ease some of the ideological challenges, a transformative dual-price system was established. Under this system, there was an official price under which SOEs operated, and a market price under which private enterprises conducted their operations. The former was higher, and it operated as a cushion to reduce potential harmful effects that sudden price changes might bring. As expected, the dual-price system encountered a substantial amount of fraud and was later abandoned. During this first stage of reform, the country moved like a checkers game, two steps forwards followed by one step backwards (Nolan, 2001). In the midst of this period, the 1989 Tiananmen tragedy occurred, and the country was again isolated from the rest of the world.

Following Deng Xiaoping's south China visit in 1992, the country was reconnected to the world economy, and its economic reform was rekindled. In 1993, another landmark reform labelled 'privatisation' appeared as an extension of the earlier reforms. In the context of this book, the most significant change of this reform was the removal of socio-economic burdens (education, healthcare, pension, etc.) from China's SOEs to different levels of the government. From that point on, China's SOEs began their long march to global eminence.

2.3   FIRM REFORMS

2.3.1   *The First Wave of SOE Reforms (1993–2001)*

China's SOEs have long been the crown jewels of the nation. As such, they enjoy unwavering financial resources and political support. However, they were poorly governed, and by 1993 many of them had devolved into highly inefficient economic black holes. In 1993, these SOEs underwent the progressive and overlapping waves of reforms. Many inefficient SOEs, irrespective of size, were closed down, merged, or acquired by their economically efficient counterparts. As an example, Haier was reborn as part of this first wave of reform (see the discussion later in this chapter on Haier's success).

The unprecedented restructuring in the SOEs caused lay-offs of more than 43 million workers and a widespread unemployment rate of 12 per cent. If this happened to other nations with no safety net for unemployment, the situation would likely be unbearable. In China, a good portion of the burden of unemployment was relieved by the financial support of family members. Interestingly, many unemployed workers became entrepreneurs and started small business operations.

2.3.2   *Privately Owned Firms: China's New Growth Engine*

The massive and painful reforms did have some silver linings. First, many SOEs in key and strategic sectors were streamlined and forced to learn to operate within their economic means. Indeed, with government aid supporting policies and scale economy in their production, many of them begin to incorporate modern company practices (e.g., quality circles from Japan) and governance structures (joint stock companies). Second, the number of entrepreneurs and small businesses increased throughout the country. These small firms grabbed market niches unreached by the SOEs, and, by learning from foreign and overseas Chinese firms, they started to become salient pillars that supported China's economy during the transitional years.

Whereas the share of SOEs in the economy subsided (Figure 2.2), private firms grew by leaps and bounds. By 2003, private firms contributed more than 50 per cent of the country's GDP and national employment. Their growth was partly helped by the closing down of inefficient SOEs. Over time, the number of 'central-government' SOEs has declined from 196 in 2003 to 115 in March 2013 (Gang and Hope, 2015).

By 2012, the national share of industrial output by SOEs was down to 26 per cent, while the share of urban employment by SOEs was reduced to 18 per cent. In 2013, SOEs accounted for only 11 per cent of China's exports, compared to 47 per cent by foreign firms and 39 per cent by domestic private firms. Nonetheless, SOEs, including those owned by provincial and municipal governments, still accounted for 34 per cent of total fixed investment, compared with 48 per cent by private firms (and the remainder by governments at all levels; Cooper, 2014).

Huawei, Lenovo, and Alibaba are the exemplars of Chinese private enterprises, and they are indeed the cream of the crop.

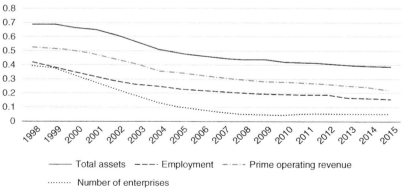

FIGURE 2.2 Share of SOEs in China's economy
Source: China Statistical Yearbook (2016)

Nonetheless, there are many others and by 2012 China had 10.9 million private companies (with 113 million employees) and 40.4 million individual enterprises (employing 86.3 million people). This rapid expansion of private enterprises has no parallel in other countries nor in China's economic history (Cooper, 2014). Compared with the SOEs, these private firms are more innovative, export-oriented, and adaptive to changing environments. As will be discussed later, they are highly active globally. As expected, the return on assets of private firms in the industrial sector exceeded that of the SOEs by about three to one (Gang and Hope, 2015). It is likely that the incentives in private firms have motivated their workers and managers to operate more effectively than SOEs.

2.3.3   State Capitalism: China's Unique Economic Model

From 1979 to 2014, China's economy grew robustly, with an annual real GDP that averaged around 10 per cent. This translates to a real GDP jump of twenty-five-fold since the reforms began in 1979. By 2014, China had become the world's second largest economy. This unprecedented performance has attracted intense attention, and researchers and policymakers attribute this economic success to China's unique government-business model.

Labelled either as 'network capitalism' (Boisot and Child, 1996) or as 'state-capitalism' (Bremmer, 2009), researchers attribute China's economic success to how its SOEs operate and are supported. Some have shown that these SOEs obtain financial capital at low costs (Qian, 2000), receive favourable policies (Luo and Peng, 1999), and leverage government ties to boost their performance (Gu, Hung, and Tse, 2008). Luo and Tung (2007) pointed out that SOEs from China have expanded in unconventional ways. Using any available resources (government, internal, and external) as springboards, Chinese firms have expanded at an amazing speed. Most studies published in the twentieth century adopted a negative lens towards SOEs, highlighting how these firms violated free market behaviours (Boisot and Child, 1996).

However, studies published in recent years noted that the capabilities of Chinese firms (both private firms and SOEs) have dramatically improved (Lau, Tse, and Zhou, 2002). They have acquired new capabilities (Tan and Tan, 2005) and capitalised on opportunities by benefitting from economic and social directives set by the government (Bremmer, 2009). In exchange, they receive from the government financial supports, preferential treatment, and policies that tilted to their favour (Tse, Yu, and Zhu, 2017). This form of state-assisted capitalism has proven to be highly effective and helped to make China the world's second largest economy (Economist, 2012).

This state-capitalistic model operates effectively in China's SOEs. As a result, it helps its SOEs to rebound and contribute to China's GDP. While the SOEs' contribution fell from 50 per cent in 1998 to 25 per cent in 2011, the unique 'state-capitalism' model allowed them to bounce back. By 2015, their share of industrial output gradually increased to over 40 per cent. In addition, 43 per cent of profits in China came from companies in which the state owned majority interests.

2.4 ENTRY INTO WORLD TRADE ORGANISATION AND GLOBALISATION

Since 1979, foreign firms have been allowed to operate as joint venture partners with minority interests in China. Beginning with China's entry into the World Trade Organisation (WTO) in 2001, foreign firms were able to operate as wholly owned firms. As a result, many researchers regard globalisation as another phase of reform in China's modern economy. To align with WTO requirements, many closed and fragmented markets in China were opened to private and international competition. This reform transformed China from the 'world factory' to the 'world market' and sparked a global rush of foreign direct investments (FDIs) into China.

Within a few years, all Fortune Global 500 firms were operating in China (McKinsey Quarterly, 2010), and, by 2008, more than 2,000 global firms had set up research and development centres in the country. This unprecedented rush of investment, talent, and technology has led to positive spillovers that boosted the competence of China's private and state-owned firms. For private firms, WTO requirements presented them with an opportunity to access China's once restricted markets. In addition, the new wave of international firms entering China showcased their latest product designs and technology for these firms to emulate.

To Chinese SOEs, whose competence have been strengthened through two decades of reforms, this new wave of competition forced them to consider going global. Some analysts had predicted that the opening of China's restricted markets would cause many SOEs to fail. Instead, the robust growth of the Chinese economy has benefitted both foreign and local firms. Furthermore, by learning from their global competitors, most Chinese firms continue to prosper. In 2005, China's central government encouraged Chinese firms to globalise. In the decade that followed, Chinese firms began their global march to become emerging market MNCs.

2.4.1   Globalisation of Chinese Firms

As Table 2.2 shows, Chinese firms operated beyond the Chinese mainland as early as the late 1970s. Some of them were listed in the Hong Kong Stock Exchange, activities that were partly designed to prepare Hong Kong's return to China in 1997. After 1997, these firms continued to regard Hong Kong as their globalisation gateway; yet, these expansions were sporadic from 1999 to 2001.

China's entry to the WTO marked a bold step. Four years later, in 2005, the governmental blessing for firms to 'go abroad' was officially announced. After a decade of global expansion, many SOEs emerged as major global player in their respective industries. In the Fortune Global 500 list of year 2018, China ranked second with 120 companies, just behind the USA with 126 companies. On this list, Sinopec ranked second and China National Petroleum ranked third, surpassing Royal Dutch Shell. Similarly, the Industrial and Commercial Bank of China, ranked 26th, was the highest ranking

Table 2.2 *Development of China's MNCs in three phases*

Phases	Nature and relevance to China's MNC
Phase 1: 1978–92	**Early and tentative development**
	Recognise the legal status of overseas investments
Phase 2: 1993–2001	**Sporadic development**
	Some favourable policies were in place to facilitate MNC activities
Phase 3: 2002–present	**Stable and fast development**
	'Going-out' strategy was implemented
	Regulatory activities were strengthened

bank on the list, well ahead of BNP Paribas (ranked 44th) and JPMorgan Chase & Co. (ranked 47th) (Fortune, 2018). These results can be regarded as engineered by the Chinese government, because these SOEs are protected by government regulations and have a strong monopolistic grip in their respective industries in China.

At the same time, many Chinese private firms have also globalised. These include SMEs as well as larger firms like Fosun (which bought Club Med in April 2015) and Xiaomi (which sold 92 million cell phones globally in 2017 at a growth rate higher than Apple, Samsung, and Huawei combined; Faulkner, 2018). In addition, Baidu and Alibaba are other highly recognisable global brand names. Comparatively, private firms have shown strong growth in recent years. They benefit from strong demand in China and, through various means (e.g., mergers and acquisitions; M&As), have grown to become industry or market leaders in the world.

2.4.2   Current Globalisation Patterns of Chinese Firms

The strong growth of Chinese firms and their overseas investments have attracted global attention. Some institutions, such as American Enterprise Institute and Heritage Foundation, maintain a continuous online report on their growth and patterns.

There are three types of fund flows from China, including non-financial funds, balance of payment (i.e., most trade balance), and corporate M&As. Although non-financial outbound foreign direct investment (FDI) flows have historically been the highest among the three, corporate M&As have since soared, reaching USD228 billion, compared to USD120 billion in non-financial funds in 2017. China's FDIs rank third in the world, behind those of the USA and Japan. However, if one also includes those from Hong Kong, then the total share of Chinese FDI surpassed that of Japan and became second in the world in 2017 (Hanemann and Rosen, 2013).

The non-financial outbound FDI grew steadily over the years up to 2016 (see Figure 2.3). From a modest USD12.4 billion (in 2005), China's outbound FDI grew over thirteen-fold over the next ten years to reach its peak at USD170.1 billion (in 2016) before dropping down to USD120.1 billion (in 2017), the second highest figure. The recent slump is regarded as an adjustment to the depreciation in the yuan and the resulting governmental initiative to curb the rapid rise in capital outflow that may threaten the country's financial stability (Bloomberg News, 2018). The government's 'guiding opinions', approved in August 2017, classified outbound investments into three groups: encouraged transactions (e.g., infrastructure projects

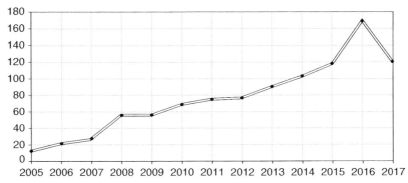

FIGURE 2.3 China's outbound FDI (in billions of USD)
Source: Ministry of Commerce (2018)

tied to the BRI, high-tech businesses, agriculture), discouraged transactions (e.g., real estate: it has caused concerns in many countries for
pushing up the price), and prohibited (e.g., gambling) (Huang and Xia,
2018). It is evident from Figure 2.3 that the guidelines have successfully slowed down the growth in outbound FDI and better align it with
the country's strategy. The issues of investing in the BRI and high-tech
businesses will be taken up in Chapter 9 given their strategic impor-
tance to China's growth and development.

2.4.3   Myths and Facts

There are several myths regarding how and why China's FDIs invest
globally. The first myth is that they concentrate in selective industries
and in designated regions. Instead, statistics showed that their investments spread across industries and regions. From 2005 to 2014, a high
percentage of Chinese investment was in the energy-related sector
(USD305 billion), followed by the transportation (USD134 billion),
and mining sectors (USD124 billion). Among the regions that received
China's FDIs, Europe topped the list. Its share rose sharply from
18 per cent in 2013 to 53.4 per cent in 2017. This was followed by
Asia (18.8 per cent) and North America (16.0 per cent), which have
switched places from a year ago, likely as a result of the BRI as well as
rising protectionism of the US administration (Huang and Xia, 2018;
see Figure 2.4).

The second myth is that China uses its FDIs strategically to gain
an unfair advantage in some competitive sectors in the global economy. It is suggested that China ordered its SOEs to acquire mines (e.g.,
iron ores from Australia), energy-based firms (coal, oil, power plants),
or food manufacturers (farms and food processing facilities). However,
Chinese firms also invest for their corporate interests. Many of them
engaged in overseas M&A to gain market access, to grow sales, and to
acquire proprietary assets (e.g., brand names, distribution channels,
and technologies). In fact, there are various benefits for Chinese firms
that globalise their operations. First, these firms (e.g., Haier, Xiaomi)
command a higher brand premium in their home market. Chinese

FIGURE 2.4 China's global outreach
Source: Heritage Foundation (2018)

consumers regard firms that export to the EU or US markets as more advanced. As a result, they are willing to pay a higher price for their products. Second, firms with global operations receive more government support. This support is provided in two ways. China's industrial parks (e.g., Suzhou industrial park) often provide land for firms with exporting capabilities at lower costs. In addition, China's EXIM bank gives out sizable loans (e.g., RMB100 million) at a low cost (less than 5 per cent) to firms that export technology-related products to other parts of the world. In short, many Chinese firms globalise their operations for their own interests.

The third myth is that only China's SOEs engage in overseas acquisitions. Statistics, however, show that both Chinese SOEs and Chinese private firms globalise their operations. In fact, private firms are gaining momentum. Seven out of the ten major Chinese M&As in the UK in 2015 are from private firms.

2.4.4 Challenges to Globalisation

Partly because of these myths, Chinese firms' globalisation is met with suspicion and, in some cases, strong resistance. Some countries set up trade hurdles (e.g., car tyres in the US market) against exports from Chinese firms. For major infrastructures that provide growth opportunities for host markets (e.g., high-speed rails), such resistance can be substantial. In Indonesia, the USD5.5 billion high-speed rail project was put on hold one week after it began in January 2016.

For M&A, resistance is often strong if these projects source raw materials from the host nations (e.g., Australia and African countries). Some host-country citizens regard these raw materials as their national endowment and thus demand higher compensation. If the operation lies close to where people live, resettlement costs are significant. At times, environmental impacts can become highly salient issues. In sum, Chinese firms are facing higher costs and a longer negotiation process than their competitors in their overseas M&As. For example, it took two years of intense negotiation for Chinalco to purchase Rio Tinto in 2009 (Cimilluca, Oster, and Or, 2009).

Beyond the economics, the rise of China as a global economic power has started debates on its political implications, which spill over to doubts and negative sentiments against globalising Chinese firms. Some countries and institutions (e.g., the USA and EU) regard potential geopolitical implications as a high-priority issue, especially those in Africa (EuroMonitor International, 2015). How Chinese firms handle these issues will be discussed in the later part of the book.

2.4.5 Summary

Historically, Chinese firms have engaged in overseas operations in Hong Kong for decades. However, their global march is a recent phenomenon, which began in 2005 as the Chinese government endorsed the need for firms to globalise their operations. Within a decade, China's FDIs have become the third largest in the world, behind those of the USA and Japan. Indeed, Chinese firms have taken a highly visible path in their globalisation activities.

We can derive several characteristics of this transformation (from 2005 to 2018). First, the speed of growth in China's FDIs (in size, sales, or asset acquisition) is unprecedented, outpacing other nations (e.g., USA, Russia, India, etc.) Second, while these FDIs cut across different industries, the percentage is much higher in base industries like oil and materials (steel, aluminium, etc.) than others. Nonetheless, these investments are not country specific. In the first quarter of 2016, Chinese firms acquired USD16.5 billion (Shi, 2016) in overseas assets in thirty-six countries and across fifteen industries. Third, there are mixed reasons underlying Chinese firms' globalisation. It reflects both a proactive orientation tailored to advance China's future development and a reactive orientation as Chinese firms seek opportunities to continue to grow. While most Chinese SOEs assume a proactive strategy, private firms globalise for their corporate needs.

Chinese firms are risk-takers in their global expansion, and their geographic reach surprises many analysts. From Asia to Africa and Oceania and from Europe to the Americas, their footprints have now reached six continents. In so doing, they adopt various globalisation strategies and models. As Luo and Tung (2007) pointed out, some of these firms use unconventional models that defy established theories. In the next two chapters, we will discuss four models of their globalisation in detail with selected firms as examples.

However, Chinese firms are far from being experienced globalisers, and they face both internal and external challenges. The internal issues include managing diversity (i.e., gender, culture, and aspirations), developing local talent, and maintaining sustainable operations in different host countries. Externally, these firms face challenges in positioning their brands, cultivating positive public images and meeting host-country demands. More significantly, few Chinese firms are able to exploit the full potential of being global companies. Up to this point, these globalised Chinese firms have not synergised their value chains, nor have they integrated their locational and firm-specific advantages effectively. We shall discuss these issues in later chapters.

REFERENCES

Bloomberg News. (2018). China's Outbound Investment Slumped in 2017 as Deals Scrutinized. *Bloomberg News*. 16 January. Retrieved 2 July 2019. www.bloom berg.com/news/articles/2018-01-16/china-s-outbound-investment-slumped-in -2017-as-deals-scrutinized.

Boisot, M. and Child, J. (1996). From fiefs to clans and network capitalism: explaining China's emerging economic order. *Administrative Science Quarterly*, 41(4): 600–28.

Bremmer, I. (2009). State Capitalism Comes of Age. *Foreign Affairs*, May/ June: 1–11.

China Statistical Yearbook. (2016). Retrieved 2 July 2019. www.stats.gov.cn/tjsj/ ndsj/2016/indexeh.

Cimilluca, D., Oster, S., and Or, A. (2009). Rio Tinto Scuttles Its Deal with Chinalco. *Wall Street Journal*. 5 June 5. Retrieved 2 July 2019. www.wsj.com /articles/SB124411140142684779.

Cooper, R. (2014). China's Growing Private Sector. *Caixin*. 30 October. Retrieved 2 July 2019. http://english.caixin.com/2014-10-30/100744910.html.

Deng, K. (2014). From economic failure to economic reforms, lessons from China's modern growth, 1949 to 2012. *Groniek*, 199: 141–61.

Economist. (2012). The Visible Hand. *Economist*. 21 January. Retrieved 2 July 2019. www.economist.com/special-report/2012/01/21/the-visible-hand.

EuroMonitor International. (2015). China. Retrieved 2 July 2019. www .euromonitor.com/china.

Faulkner, C. (2018). Xiaomi Grew More in 2017 than Apple, Samsung and Huawei Combined. *Techradar*, 2 February. Retrieved 2 July 2019. www.techradar.com /news/xiaomi-grew-more-in-2017-than-apple-samsung-and-huawei-combined.

Fortune. (2018). Global 500. *Fortune*. Retrieved 2 July 2019. http://fortune.com/gl obal500/list/.

Gang, F. and Hope, N. (2015). The Role of State-Owned Enterprises in the Chinese Economy. *US-China 2022: Economic Relations in the Next 10 Years*. Chapter 16. Retrieved 2 July 2019. www.chinausfocus.com/2022/index-page_id=1480 .html.

Gu, F. F., Hung, K., and Tse, D. K. (2008). When does guanxi matter? Issues of capitalization and its dark sides. *Journal of Marketing*, 72(4): 12–28.

Hanemann, T. and Rosen, D. H. (2013). China's Reform Era and Outward Investment. *Rhodium Group*. 2 December. Retrieved 2 July 2019. https://rhg.com/research/chinas-reform-era-and-outward-investment/.

Heritage Foundation. (2018). China Global Investment Tracker, electronic dataset. *AEI*. Retrieved 2 July 2019. www.aei.org/china-global-investment-tracker/.

Huang, B. and Xia, L. (2018). China | ODI from the Middle Kingdom: What's Next after the Big Turnaround? *BBVA Research*. February. Retrieved 2 July 2019. www.bbvaresearch.com/wp-content/uploads/2018/02/201802_ChinaWatch_China-Outward-Investment_EDI.pdf.

Lau, C.-M., Tse, D. K., and Zhou, N. (2002). Institutional forces and organizational culture in China: effects on change schemas, firm commitment and job satisfaction. *Journal of International Business Studies*, 33(3): 533–50.

Luo, Y. and Peng, M. W. (1999). Learning to compete in a transition economy: experience, environment, and performance. *Journal of International Business Studies*, 30(2): 269–95.

Luo, Y. and Tung, R. L. (2007). International expansion of emerging market enterprises: a springboard perspective. *Journal of International Business Studies*, 38(4): 481–98.

McKinsey Quarterly. (2010). Executive summary. *McKinsey Quarterly*.

Ministry of Commerce. (2018). *Statistical Bulletin of China's Outward Foreign Direct Investment*. Beijing: China Statistics Press.

Nolan, P. (2001). *China and the Global Economy*. Basingstoke: Palgrave.

Shi, J. (2016). Record Quarter for Outbound M&As. *China Daily*. 19 April. Retrieved 2 July 2019. http://europe.chinadaily.com.cn/business/2016-04/29/content_24970484.htm.

Tan, J. and Tan, D. (2005). Environment-strategy co-evolution and co-alignment: a staged model of Chinese SOEs under transition. *Strategic Management Journal*, 26: 141–57.

Tse, C. H., Yu, L., and Zhu, J. (2017). A multimediation model of learning by exporting: Analysis of export-induced productivity gains. *Journal of Management*, 43(7): 2118–46.

United Nations. (2018). National accounts, GDP and GDP per capita, electronic dataset. *UN data*. Retrieved 2 July 2019. http://data.un.org/Default.aspx.

3 Globalisation of Chinese Firms Using Existing Paradigms

3.1 INTRODUCTION

By 2015, after a decade of globalisation practices, the footprints of Chinese firms had reached all regions of the world. Indeed, the global rise of Chinese firms has surpassed all forecasts and expectations. Their successes and speed of globalisation are unparalleled in corporate history. As Chapter 2 pointed out, several complex and unique incidents gave rise to the Chinese economy as a world power and its globalising firms. Some scholars attributed the firms' success to the country's successful and overlapping reforms. Others framed it as collusive actions between the government and firms (e.g., Walder, 1995). Still others attributed it to the uniqueness of state capitalism (Bremmer, 2009). Nevertheless, many remain doubtful regarding whether the firms' phenomenal growth can be sustained.

In 2001, China made a concerted effort to enter the global arena by joining the WTO. This landmark step allowed foreign firms to operate wholly owned subsidiaries in the country. On the one hand, it encouraged many global firms to enter China, building R&D centres and designing new products tailored to the growing China market. On the other hand, the rush of global competition forced China's SOEs and private firms to become globally competent. It compelled them to develop overseas markets for their products. By now, many of China's top SOEs rank among leading firms in sales and in profit. In 2015, three of them entered Fortune's top ten list. Private firms that have shown strong growth in recent years have also joined the ranks of top companies in their respective industries and begun their global expansion.

This chapter discusses how Chinese firms globalise their operations using classic globalisation models. It discusses two firms, Haier and Chalco, whose fundamental motivations, strategic moves, and operational characteristics exemplify Chinese SOEs. The discussion provides indicative insights on the rising roles of Chinese firms in the global economy. How Chinese firms adopt newer models of globalisation will be discussed in Chapter 4.

3.2   THEORIES OF INTERNATIONAL BUSINESS

Before going into specific details of the globalising firms' strategies, it is useful to review the classic view on international business and how it has evolved into modern globalisation models for Chinese firms.

3.2.1   From International Trade to International Business: Cost–Advantage Paradigm

For decades, scholars have adopted the cost–advantage paradigm to understand the origins and patterns of trade across nations. Simply put, if two countries each produce a particular product at a lower cost than if that product is produced in the other country, the two countries would be better off producing more of the same product, export the excess output, and import the other product from the other country. Thus, if Country A produces Product 'a' cheaper and Country B produces Product 'b' cheaper, Country A should produce more 'a', sell the excess and buy 'b' from Country B (and vice versa). Through product specialisation and trade, both countries will be better off economically, using fewer resources for the same economic result, provided that the transportation and other transactional costs do not take away the gains in more efficient production. More than fifty years of research efforts on various costs (e.g., raw material, commodity, labour, capital equipment, financial capital) and cost-related constructs (labour and capital productivity, transportation and logistics) have substantiated the cost–advantage paradigm.

Today, production in the global economy has expanded into a highly complex, multinational, value-chain ecosystem. In the globalisation era, where the world is increasingly 'flat' as a result of ever-declining communication, transportation and production costs, the essence of the original cost–advantage view remains central to the understanding of how global businesses are conducted. Conceptually, the cost–advantage view offers a rich platform for other firm theories, such as transactional-cost theory and the resource-based view, to build on. It is also the most common starting point for managers and government policymakers to make decisions on trade-related policies. China was labelled the 'world factory', this label in itself reflects how the cost–advantage view dominates discussion to this day.

3.2.2   MNCs as International Business Players

In spite of the dominance of the cost–advantage paradigm, there is a significant change in the operational nature of international trade, which is no longer controlled by nations. Instead, most if not all of our global businesses are corporatised – conducted by firms with complex networks and organisational levels. It is not an overstatement to say that most of today's international trade and businesses are in the hands of firms governed by corporate leaders, who are more responsive to their shareholders' benefits than to national needs. In addition, the corporate leaders are faced with different missions, goals, operating systems, and management cultures that they are obliged to comply with, and to position their firms in the most profitable part of the value chain to capitalise on the cost advantages in the global economy. A good example is Nike, a company in which the design is conducted in the USA, while the production of its products (millions of pairs of shoes and sportswear articles) are outsourced to supply chain partners whose operating units are located in countries with the lowest costs.

Run by corporate leaders and their boards of directors, these firms range from being highly entrepreneurial and innovative (e.g., Apple, Samsung) to being cautious and stable (e.g., BP, P&G). Some corporate leaders are semi-governmental officials whose duties are defined by their respective governments. An example would be China's SOEs. Collectively, these private and state-owned firms determine much of today's global economy. By now, some global firms are so large that their annual sales surpass those of nations or regions. For example, Walmart's global sales of USD476.3 billion rank just behind Chinese Taiwan's GDP, which would make Walmart the world's top twenty-eighth economy. Moreover, all of the top ten Fortune 500 firms have sales higher than the GDP of Portugal, which ranks forty-sixth in the world. External to the firms, social, economic, and political forces as well as public policies set up by host and home countries are salient institutional drivers that shape how these global firms behave.

3.2.3 Understanding MNCs' Global Operations

The most well-known model to understand how MNCs (also called multinational enterprises) operate is Dunning's OLI (Ownership, Locational, and Internationalisation) Model of firm internationalisation (Dunning, 1988). The model builds upon and extends the original cost–advantage view. Rather than using cost differentials across countries as the only reason for international business, Dunning's model postulates that firms also leverage their *ownership advantages* (e.g., brand name, proprietary technologies), *locational advantages* (e.g., sourcing low material, capital, and talent costs in various countries), and *internationalisation advantages* (e.g., gaining innovative insights globally, levering global status as brand premium, balancing operating risks) as determinants of MNC operation and growth. By combining some or all of these advantages, MNCs will be able to enjoy competitive advantages over their competitors and maximise their profits.

3.2.4 Firm Globalisation as a Process

The OLI model is highly comprehensive, because it covers all key domains of firm competitive advantages. Over time, several major contributions of the model are recognised. First, it posits firm *globalisation as a process* (rather than a single act or decision). Second, it notes that *the globalising process is eclectic* in nature, allowing the firm to choose between transactions in the open market and carry out internal transactions at lower costs. Third, the model recognises *globalisation as complex interplays* involving a firm's ownership, locational, and international advantages.

As an overarching model, *OLI effectively synthesises strands of specific theories* on firm behaviour, including international trade theory (Vernon, 1966), the competitive advantage view (Grant, 1991), the resource-based view (Barney, 1991), transactional cost theory (Williamson, 1979), and social institutional theory (Scott, 1995). However, the OLI is a generalised model and does not prescribe the motives that drive specific firm internationalisation behaviour. For example, when a Chinese firm's board of directors discusses whether it should enter India, the discussion would likely cover considerations of ownership advantages (what advantage does our firm have that can be leveraged in India?), country advantages (what about India is attractive to our company?), and internationalisation advantages (will the Indian operations enhance our firm as a whole?). After these strategic issues are considered and evaluated, the firm's final decision to enter India may turn into actionable elements, including (1) what entry mode will enable the firm to capitalise on the advantages of the Indian operation (thus, transactional cost theory applies); and (2) whether the Indian operation should be stage-wise so that the expected benefits will not be compromised by the firm's lack of experience (thus, organisational learning applies) or whether the India operation can fully imitate the China operation. In the following sections, we discuss the globalisation of two exemplary Chinese firms (Haier and Chalco).

3.3   HAIER: A LEGENDARY EXAMPLE OF THE COST–ADVANTAGE GLOBALISATION MODEL

Among the early globalisation successes by Chinese firms, the most famous example is Haier. In 1984, Haier was a non-performing factory in Qingdao in north-eastern China, producing substandard refrigerators (about eighty per month) that consumers largely ignored. The firm was at the brink of bankruptcy when Mr Zhang Ruimin, a former factory manager, took over and revived the firm. Under Zhang's leadership,

Table 3.1 *Top five home appliance brands*

Rank	2006	2012	2018
1	Haier (China)	Haier (China)	Haier (China)
2	Whirlpool (USA)	Whirlpool (USA)	Electrolux (Sweden)
3	LG Electronics (South Korea)	Electrolux (Sweden)	LG Electronics (South Korea)
4	GE (USA)	Gree Electric (China)	Whirlpool (USA)
5	Electrolux (Sweden)	BSH Bosch & Siemens (Germany)	Samsung Electronics (South Korea)

Source: Top 5 of Anything (2019)

Haier became the world's largest 'white goods' (i.e., household appliance) manufacturer in 2008, a position it has held since then. By 2017, Haier owned a 10.6 per cent market share and generated an annual global revenue of USD37.2 billion. Zhang has been a frequent speaker at the World Knowledge Forum and other podiums since 2000, sharing his experience on how he revived and globalised Haier. Table 3.1 lists the top home appliance brands in 2006, 2012, and 2018, indicating Haier's resilience in the face of rapid changes in the industry.

3.3.1   First Phase in Haier's Revival: Technology, Product Quality, and Organisational Learning

Zhang turned around Haier in several ways. He started by tracing customers' complaints and understanding why Haier refrigerators broke down quickly. He uncovered that 20 per cent of the factory's output had functional problems, and he instructed that all thirty-six refrigerators in the inventory (each costing a worker's salary for two years) be destroyed. After destroying the inventory, Zhang insisted that only quality products would be allowed to leave the factory. He enforced this by instituting a stringent quality standard in the production process. To improve production quality, Haier formed a joint venture with the German refrigerator company Liebherr. Through Liebherr's help, Haier gained much-needed production technology. Equipped with this new know-how, Zhang engaged the entire firm to follow quality production processes similar to the famous quality circle in top Japanese firms like Panasonic. His move proved to be a success that improved Haier's production both qualitatively and quantitatively.

Externally, Zhang faced an equally formidable challenge, because Chinese consumers had limited consumption power and held a poor impression of locally made products. Zhang increased the firm's advertising and public relations efforts. More significantly, Haier adopted some unconventional promotional efforts, such as publicity stunts. In market squares where people gathered, Haier displayed its products and then dropped an item (e.g., a 30-lb Haier hotwater boiler for household use) from a 10-metre platform. After the drop, Haier staff reconnected the boiler and showed surrounding consumers that the product still functioned properly. These publicity stunts attracted large crowds and media coverage. Gradually, consumers were persuaded of Haier's superior product quality compared to other local firms. Within two years, by 1986, Haier was able to become profitable.

3.3.2 Second Phase in Haier's Revival: From an Accidental Garbage Collector to China's Pride

From 1984 to 2000, Haier's sales multiplied by 115 times, reaching RMB40.5 billion (from RMB3.5 million in 1984). This unprecedented growth was driven by the Qingdao government. As Haier continued to outperform its competitors, Zhang was asked to absorb other ailing appliance manufacturers, including those producing washing machines (Qingdao Red Star Electronics Company), air conditioners (Qingdao Air Conditioner Plant), microwave ovens (Qingdao Electroplating Company), and freezers (Qingdao Freezer). These forced marriages gave rise to various types of problems, but Zhang and his top management team were able to turn around the failing firms. They quickly instilled the new culture of quality, transferred Haier's production technology, and then branded the improved products with the

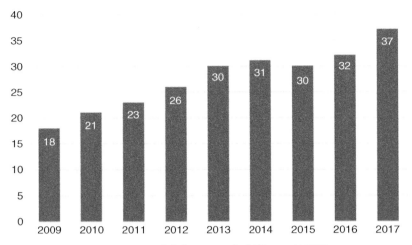

FIGURE 3.1 Haier's global revenue (in billions of USD)
Source: Haier Group (2019)

Haier name. With much-improved quality and a new brand name, these products grabbed consumers' attention and confidence. While the challenges were difficult, these M&As broadened Haier's revenue streams, enhanced its scale economy, and elevated it from being a regional to a national brand (see Figure 3.1).

Acquiring and turning around ailing firms required substantial financial resources. In all cases, Zhang bargained successfully with the Qingdao government and other governments and received loans, subsidies, and tax breaks to finance the M&A. In the early years, most of Haier's shares were owned collectively (i.e., its employees owned the majority of its stock), so Zhang did not need to justify potential losses in corporate value in these 'forced' M&As. Instead, the employees were highly motivated to ensure the M&As performed well. Haier expanded its production facilities aggressively to meet its ever-growing product demands (annual sales grew by 300 per cent). By 2000, the firm had five talent-development facilities and large-scale production plants.

Haier's growth story also helped to attract another type of resource: technology and management talents. With its high-speed

growth, Zhang was able to acquire cutting-edge technology from foreign firms through joint ventures and technology-transfer licenses. In
so doing, Haier became a legend in China. These new resources
enabled the firm to continuously develop new markets and extend
the Haier brand. The foundation of a corporate empire was laid.

Haier's phenomenal success was featured in a 1995 Harvard
Business School case. By 2000, Zhang became China's first corporate
speaker in global business, economics and entrepreneurial forums.
With well-orchestrated promotion campaigns, including building an
iconic exhibition centre in Qingdao and sponsoring an animated film
featuring Haier as a child and his adventure travelling overseas, the
firm has become the pride of China.

3.3.3   Third Phase in Haier's Revival: Being China's First Global Brand

Haier started its overseas operations as early as 1996. It opened
production units sequentially in Indonesia, the Philippines, and
Malaysia as well as Thailand. All production facilities have done
well, but the brand failed in Malaysia. In the US market, the firm
adopted a conservative route, putting its name only on compact
refrigerators and electric wine cellars. The bulk of its production
capacity (e.g., big refrigerators and other large household appliances) was devoted to original equipment manufacturer (OEM)
orders by US firms.

The year 2000 was a landmark year for Haier, in that the
firm opened its production facilities for full-sized refrigerators in
Camden, South Carolina, USA, and, by 2002, it generated
USD200 million in sales. This successful globalisation experience has led to a quick proliferation of other overseas operations,
including operations in Pakistan (2002), Jordan (2003), India
(2005), and subsequently in five African countries (Tunisia,
Nigeria, Egypt, Algeria, and South Africa). It also formed joint
ventures with local firms in Venezuela. (Khanna, Palepu, and
Andrews, 2011).

How profitable these early global attempts were is unknown; nonetheless, the move had a strong effect in China. Haier was the first Chinese brand to meet the quality standard demanded by high-income American consumers (whose average income was more than twenty times that of Chinese consumers in 2000). This intensified a strong 'China pride' among its domestic consumers and elevated Haier's brand premium above those of other local brands (Haier's products charge 15 per cent higher) with impressive sales volume.

Haier began acquiring other brands, such as Meneghetti in Italy, as early as 2001. In June 2005, it recognised the need to improve its brand image. Backed by private equity funds Blackstone Group and Bain Capital, Haier made a bid to acquire the famous Maytag Corporation. The bid was for USD1.28 billion, or USD16 per share, topping a competitive offer by Ripplewood Holdings (USD14.26 a share). However, its bid was surpassed by Whirlpool Corporation which offered USD21 per share. In 2012, Haier Group bought the New Zealand appliance manufacturing company Fisher & Paykel. Haier's share in the global large household appliance market soared during this period (Figure 3.2).

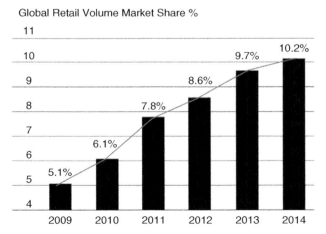

FIGURE 3.2 Haier's market share, 2009–14
Source: Haier Group (2019)

3.3.4   A Household Legend

Haier has successfully leveraged its advantages as a collectively owned company and gained strong government support. With this background, Haier did not have to fully disclose its globalisation or M&A plans to all shareholders. This advantage is also critical to other highly successful Chinese firms (e.g., Huawei) and emerging giants (e.g., Alibaba before its public listing). However, Haier faced a major limitation, in that it lacked the financial resources to grow outside of China, where exchange controls have been tight. To mitigate this issue, Haier listed two of its operations: Qingdao Haier Refrigerator Co. on the Shanghai Stock Exchange in 1993 (valued at USD9.9 billion in February 2015) and Haier Electric (a joint venture) on the Hong Kong Stock Exchange in 2005 (valued at USD6.99 billion in February 2015). The two listings enabled the firm to bypass currency hurdles that the Chinese government imposes on most firms.

Euromonitor reported in 2008 that Haier had surpassed Whirlpool as the world's top refrigerator producer by sales (Feng, 2016) with high profit margin. Haier said it had sold 12 million refrigerators worldwide, an increase of 20 per cent from 2007. Its market share reached 6.3 per cent globally. By 2011, Haier was recognised as one of the world's top five white goods manufacturers. In 2014, it achieved its goal of being the world's largest white goods manufacturer, commanding 10.2 per cent of the world market. Currently, Haier employs 70,000 employees, and its 2014 sales reached USD32.8 billion, generating a profit of USD2.45 billion (adapted from Haier Group History, 2019).

3.3.5   A Summary of the Case of Haier

Haier's legendary achievement is unprecedented in several ways. First, Haier is in a highly mature and challenging appliance market dominated by global firms from the USA (GE, Whirlpool, Maytag), Japan (Sharp, Toshiba, Hitachi), and Europe. Second, it does not have any cutting-edge or disruptive technology that enables the firm to challenge the established giants. Third, it has had to carry and revive several large and failed firms in Qingdao rather than start anew. Fourth, it has had to gingerly balance its relationship with the provincial government in the midst of overlapping phases of reforms in China during which policy changes were rapid and market demand was volatile.

Despite these challenges, Zhang's change leadership has been instrumental in building Haier's corporate empire. According to Dunning's OLI globalisation model, the firm has *ownership advantages* that include entrepreneurship skills by Zhang, unwavering government support, and the status of a collectively owned firm (owned by both government and employees). It also has *locational advantage* (China's high demand growth, low production costs, large talent pools). Further, by going abroad, Haier gained an *internationalisation advantage* as China's first global brand (thus elevating Haier's brand premium at home) and leveraged China's market size for cutting-edge technology from leading firms. It also gained financial freedom by publicly listing the firm in Hong Kong to bypass China's home-policy hurdles.

One could attribute Haier's rise to several unique causes. First, during its rise, most of the global competitors (Maytag, Sharp, etc.) were relaxed, neglecting the high growth potentials in China. Rather than matching or counteracting Haier's low-price strategy, they chose to maintain a high-margin strategy, leaving the low-end China market (and other emerging markets) to Haier. Second, China's three decades of robust economic growth (1980–2010) surprised all global firms. This robust growth has led to a steady development of highly efficient supply chains across many products in China (as pointed out in Chapter 2). The combination of relaxed global competition, rising home market demand, and declining costs provide exceptional growth opportunities to Haier and other Chinese household appliance firms (like TCL, Hisense, and BBK). Undeniably, however, Mr Zhang deserves respect as a global change leader in the corporate world. He was able to consistently find successful growth paths for Haier in a complex and volatile environment. Under his leadership, Haier seized opportunities strategically and implemented its plan prudently to achieve a phenomenal performance. As Mr Jack Welch received the credit for turning GE around, Zhang Ruimin has achieved similar, if not even greater, results in an emerging market environment.

3.4 CHALCO: AN EXEMPLAR FIRM THAT RESPONDED TO NATIONAL NEED THROUGH GLOBALISATION

The three decades of robust economic growth of the world's most populous economy have placed a huge, unparalleled demand on raw material and resources. As China becomes the manufacturing platform for the world's low-price consumer markets, the country is the de facto supplier for other emerging economies (84 per cent of the world's population), whose demand has long been neglected by established MNCs. In addition, the Chinese people, representing around 25 per cent of the world's population, have strong consumption needs.

The demand for materials and resources has surged in all industries, including oil and other energy-related resources (e.g., coal, natural gases), mineral ores (e.g., steel, copper), fertilisers (organic and chemical), production-related resources (lumber, rare earth), animal feeds (corn, peas, hay), and human food (flour, rice, corn, sugar, fish, meat). The demand has been so strong and universal that almost all commodities have experienced a continuous rise in prices. During the decade of 2002–12, China's economy was growing fast at an average of 10 per cent annually; yet, the country's consumption of energy and metals tripled. By 2012, China accounts for sizable shares of world consumption in these commodities, especially in coal (50 per cent) and metals (42 per cent) (Table 3.2). Also, partly fuelled by demand and partly fuelled by speculative investments, the price of most commodities jumped by over 300 per cent between 1998 and 2012 (Figure 3.3).

Recognising the trend of rising prices and its potential impacts on China's economy, the Chinese government urged its SOEs to globalise their operations in 2005. Chinese SOEs, especially those in

Table 3.2 *China's commodity consumption (as share of world consumption) in 2012*

Commodity	China consumption (percentage of world consumption)
Primary energy	21.9
Crude oil	11.2
Coal	50.4
Metals	42.9
Grains	22.8
Edible oils	20.2
GDP	*10.0*
Industrial production	*19.1*

Source: World Bank (2015)

Price indices, constant (2010=100)

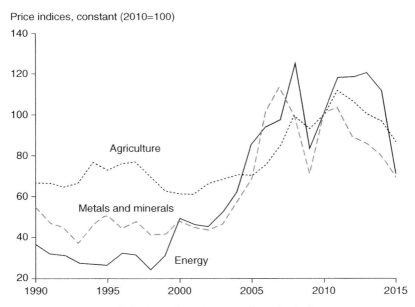

FIGURE 3.3 Inflation-adjusted commodity price indexes, 1990–2015
Source: World Bank (2015)

energy, mineral resources, and raw materials, embarked on globalisation paths, acquiring firms with large holdings of raw materials and those with mining and excavation technology. This gave rise to another firm globalisation model. Rather than pursuing business profit as in Dunning's OLI model, China's SOEs globalise their operations for a different purpose, to meet the need of a growing nation.

To fill the needs of a growing nation has been a goal for China's gas companies for quite some time. Sino Petroleum and Petro-China are owned by the state government, and their operations have been driven by both profit and national need. Under normal circumstances, they operate in the free market, following the global supply and demand in the oil industry. The gas prices in China would be closely linked to international prices. However, when there is an eminent national need (e.g., sudden rise in global gas prices from 2003 to 2008 when the price jumped from USD40 to 140), the two firms charge the retail price of gas in China below their costs to support China's national interests. The firms would expect the government to compensate their losses through special government contracts, subsidies, and other means later. In short, these two firms are operating under a flexible mixed firm-national model. Following the same vein, Chalco's national development globalisation model is a good representation of this model. In the following sections, we discuss Chalco as an interesting example of this globalisation model.

3.4.1   Background of Chalco

The Aluminum Corporation of China Limited (Chalco) is China's largest alumina and primary aluminium producer as well as the world's second largest alumina producer (Chalco, 2019). The firm was established on 10 September 2001 by merging Aluminum Corporation of China (Chinalco), Guangxi Investment (Group) Company Limited, and Guizhou Provincial Materials Development and Investment Corporation. As an SOE, Chalco was listed on the New York Stock Exchange and the Hong Kong Stock Exchange in December 2001. In 2007, Chalco was further listed as A-share on the

Shanghai Stock Exchange after acquiring additional local firms in that year. By 2015, Chalco has 240,000 employees and operated sixty-five subsidiaries in more than twenty countries.

3.4.2   Growth and Industrial Reorganisation (2001–2003)

Chalco was established as a joint-stock company co-owned by its employees, the Chinese government, and some private shareholders. By merging three regional aluminium-related mineral firms, it aimed to achieve two goals: enhancing the competitiveness of Chinese aluminum producers and transforming the country's aluminium firms into a sustainable business. This was especially important after China entered the WTO, when local firms were small and inter-firm rivalry would lead to severe price competition, hurting the nation's aluminium-producing capabilities. By using Chalco to reorganise and transform the aluminium industry, China's production capacity increased, easing the import demand of aluminium. By merging the local producers, Chalco the conglomerate can better source financial capitals and aluminium ores and acquire new technology to facilitate continuous growth.

3.4.3   Consolidation and Domestic Acquisitions (2004–2006)

Subsequent to its establishment and public listing in the Hong Kong and New York stock exchanges, Chalco was able to acquire local aluminium producers, including Lanzhou Aluminum (28 per cent of interest in 2004), Fushun Aluminum Plant (2006), and Huayu Aluminum and Power (55 per cent in 2006). The firm also formed alliance partners by forming joint ventures with Chalco Zunyi Alumina and Guizhou Wujiang Hydropower Development (2006) and acquired 51 per cent of equity in Gansu Hualu Aluminum (2006). In 2008, Chalco purchased five more aluminium-processing plants and a smelter for RMB4.2 billion.

These M&A activities avoided vicious inter-firm competition in the aluminium industry in China and allowed Chalco to develop a cost-efficient value chain and production line to maintain its cost

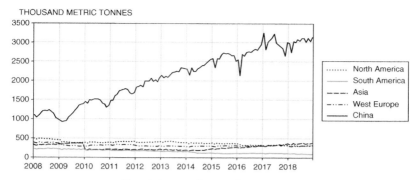

FIGURE 3.4 Aluminium production by region, 2000–18
Source: World Aluminium (2019)

advantage globally. With a downstream acquisition, Chalco is better prepared against risks when the industry goes through seasonal cycles.

These acquisition and joint venture activities proved effective. From 2001, China's aluminium production outpaced that of other global producers (Figure 3.4). During the first seven years of its establishment, Chalco's sales volume increased eight-fold (to USD30 billion), and its profits increased ten-fold. In addition, the price of aluminium had a stable hike from 2001 to 2008 (by 100 per cent), providing a reliable supply of aluminium at reasonable costs to support China's construction and car manufacturing industries.

3.4.4   Foreign Investments and Global Expansion (2005–Present)

With impressive results at both the firm and industry levels, Chalco won the government's support to allow it to play a pivotal role in China's aluminium market. Chalco's ability to effectively integrate the country's mines and production plants further strengthened the confidence of the senior management to go global. Chalco began its globalisation plan in 2005 with full endorsement from the national government.

Chalco globalised by issuing additional shares in the stock markets where it is listed. The ample resources enabled the firm to move quickly on the global stage through direct investments and capacity expansions. These included M&As, advanced technologies, overseas factory establishments, and co-operative projects with resource-rich countries. Some key projects include: a joint project with the Australian government in 2007 (Aruukum), a co-operation plan with Aricom (to develop a titanium sponge-production plant in 2007), a joint-venture with the Malaysia Mining Company (MMC), a joint venture with the Saudi Arabian Binladin Group (2008), the acquisition of Peru Copper Inc. (the firm was listed on the Toronto Stock Exchange in 2007), and the acquisition of 12 per cent of Rio Tinto through Chinalco and Alcoa Incorporated (2008). As a result, Chalco became the world's second largest aluminium producer.

Within a decade (from 2001 to 2010), Chalco transformed itself with remarkable results. It changed from a cluster of local and ineffi-cient producers with outdated technology into an economically effi-cient aluminium conglomerate with a scale economy and up-to-date technology. It also strengthened Chinese producers in the aluminium industry when China entered the WTO, thus avoiding a cut-throat price war and delivering a reliable supply of base-material supply for downstream industries. On the global front, the firm has achieved the 'impossible', becoming a global leader by leveraging financial supports from overseas markets (Table 3.3). With these remarkable results, Chalco became an exemplar firm for other SOEs to follow.

3.4.5   Celebrated Performance and an Exemplary Conglomerate

Chalco's success can be attributed to two causes. In China, it has the government's unwavering support, and it also has the resources to restructure China's aluminium industry. Going further, Chalco's lea-ders have effectively integrated the acquired firms and factories to establish a solid base for its globalisation. The capabilities of Chalco's leaders are highly commendable.

On the overseas front, Chalco's performance was equally impressive. It was able to meet regulatory requirements and be

Table 3.3 *Leading alumina producers, 2016*

1	Chalco (China)
2	Xinfa (China)
3	Hongqiao (China)
4	Rusal (Russia)
5	Rio Tinto Alcan (Canada)
6	Alcoa (USA)
7	Norsk Hydro (Norway)
8	South 32 (Australia)
9	AWC (Australia)
10	Jinjiang Group (China)

Source: AlCircle (2016)

successfully listed on overseas stock exchanges (Hong Kong and New York in 2001) and later on the Shanghai Stock Exchange (2007). In sum, the firm has succeeded in gathering both private and international financial funds to fuel its global growth.

Chalco also managed its global march in a non-confrontational manner. It did not initiate price wars to gain market shares from existing firms. Instead, it adopted a 'coopetition' relationship with its competitors. As Chalco continued to expand its production capacity, other global aluminium firms (e.g., Alcoa) also benefitted from the stable and rising global demand in aluminium with increased profits. This 'harmonious' co-operative image paid off well for the firm. It enabled Chalco to enter into stronger working relationships with resource-rich countries and technology-rich companies. To a large extent, a good portion of Chalco's projects aimed for a win–win outcome in co-exploring, co-producing, and co-marketing output with host countries. This capability is exceptional among Chinese firms, let alone SOEs.

3.4.6 Applications of the National Development Globalisation Model

Can other resource-based firms copy Chalco's strategy and globalise their operations using the same national-development model? There are several underlying criteria that must be met for this strategy to be successful. First, for the emulating firms, their corporate mission and operational plan have to align with China's national development plan in order to ensure that the firm will receive continuous government backing. As the global economy continues to fluctuate, such as during the 2008 financial crisis, support from the government (and, by extension, state-owned banks) is critical. With such unwavering supports, the emulating firms can obtain inexpensive financial resources to fuel their global growth.

Second, it is imperative that the senior management team has the management capabilities to operate in a fast-changing global economy. In this regard, Chalco's management team is outstanding. It is able to manage a diverse portfolio of firms in the aluminium value chain both within and outside of China. Internally in China, the conglomerate has demonstrated the strong ability to integrate the regional producers, capitalising on their strength. Externally, the management team has made concerted efforts to operate harmoniously with the global competitors. As a result, its global M&As faced less hostility compared with those of other firms in other industries.

Third, most of China's resource-based firms have come from a 'humble' past, lagging behind in technology and management know-how. Through joint ventures with global firms, Chalco is able to transform itself and catch up with the current technology to harvest its products. This ability to co-operate with global firms and co-develop a sustainable market reflects the strong learning capabilities within Chalco, in contrast to some Chinese firms that are aggressive and impatient in their global march. After all, the international market is very different culturally, economically, and politically from what the firms have experienced in China.

In some regards, the global aluminium market is unique, Chalco does not need a strong brand to market its products. Instead, it can focus on output quality, consistency, and reliability of delivery. This is especially true in the company's home market in China, where Chinese firms face relatively less competition.

3.4.7 Current and Future Challenges

The top challenge for Chalco is its current portfolio, which is highly reliant on aluminium. The narrow product portfolio renders the company vulnerable to business and industry cycles. Indeed, from 2009 to 2015, the production volume slowed down and with the slump in commodity prices globally, Chalco began to reports losses in 2015.

The industry's overcapacity of aluminium during the global economic crisis resulted in a drop in the company's profits by 98.7 per cent in 2008. Chalco reported RMB3.25 billion in net loss for the first half of 2012, citing falling aluminium prices and rising costs of raw materials as the causes. This alarming state of affairs led the firm to recognise the need to transform its corporate governance from a state-led to a market-led system.

As a resource-based conglomerate, Chalco needs to face increasing environmental concerns. As in the case of PetroChina, Chalco needs to maintain its role as a responsible global corporate citizenship when it operates in different host environments. In Australia, for example, a substantial portion of the public is concerned about selling their country's natural resources to foreign firms. How best to be a responsible global corporate citizen in different host economies is becoming an important issue. The ways in which Chinese firms have resolved these issues will be discussed in subsequent chapters.

REFERENCES

AlCircle. (2016). Top 10 alumina companies in the world (10 December). *AlCircle*. Retrieved 10 July 2019. www.alcircle.com/news/top-ten-alumina-companies-in-the-world-26529.

Barney, J. (1991). Firm resources and sustained competitive advantage. *Journal of Management*, 17(1): 99–120.

Bremmer, I. (2009). State Capitalism Comes of Age. *Foreign Affairs*, May/June: 1–11.

Chalco. (2019). Retrieved 23 July 2019. www.chalco.com.cn/chalcoen/index.htm/.

Dunning, J. H. (1988). The eclectic paradigm of international production: a restatement and some possible extensions. *Journal of International Business Studies*, 19(1): 1–31.

Feng, X. (2016). *On Aesthetic and Cultural Issues in Pragmatic Translation: Based on the Translation of Brand Names and Brand Slogans*. Abingdon: Routledge.

Grant, R. M. (1991). The resource-based theory of competitive advantage: implications for strategy formulation. *California Management Review*, 33(3): 114–35.

Haier Group. (2019). Retrieved 9 January 2019. www.haier.net/cnCOMP: link/.

Haier Group History. (2019). Retrieved 9 January 2019. www.haier.net/en/about_haier/history.

Khanna, T., Palepu, K., and Andrews, P. (2011). Haier: taking a Chinese company global in 2011. *Harvard Business School Strategy Unit Case*, 712–408.

Scott, W. R. (1995). *Institutions and Organizations*. Thousand Oaks, CA: Sage.

Top 5 of Anything. (2019). Top 5 major home appliance brands in the world. Retrieved 10 January 2019. https://top5ofanything.com/list/02df276c/Major -Home-Appliance-Brands-in-the-World.

Vernon, R. (1966). International investment and international trade in the product cycle. *The Quarterly Journal of Economics*, 80(2):190–207.

Walder, A. G. (1995). Local governments as industrial firms: an organizational analysis of China's transitional economy. *American Journal of Sociology*, 101 (2): 263–301.

Williamson, O. E. (1979). Transaction-cost economics: the governance of contractual relations. *Journal of Law & Economics*, 22(2): 233–61.

World Aluminium. (2019). Retrieved 1 October 2018. www.world-aluminium.org /statistics.

World Bank. (2015). How important are China and India in global commodity consumption? *Commodity Markets Outlook*. Retrieved 10 January 2019. http:// pubdocs.worldbank.org/en/716291444853736301/CMO-July-2015-Feature-China -India.pdf.

4 Globalisation of Chinese Firms Using New Paradigms

4.1 INTRODUCTION

During the past decade, China's globalisation momentum has risen at an increasing rate through the adoption of a multipronged approach. Chapter 3 discussed Dunning's globalisation (OLI) model, which allows firms, especially those in the manufacturing sector, to leverage their low-cost advantages as a base for global expansion. The OLI model is a classic approach to globalisation that has been validated across firms in many countries; however, as some Chinese firms show, the paths to globalisation are diverse and highly innovative. As a result, new globalisation models emerge from their experiences.

This chapter discusses several of these emerging models: the springboard model, its variant the leapfrog model, and the mixed model, a hybrid globalisation path that leverages the combined benefits of administrative and market systems. The most distinctive feature of the firms adopting the new paradigm models is that they do *not* possess competitive advantages globally; in short, they are defying the conventional wisdom that suggests that weak firms should not globalise.

This situation leads to several intriguing questions. How can non-competitive firms expand globally? On what bases can they gain shareholders' or investors' support to go global? How did they begin? Can their growth be sustained?

To begin to answer these questions, one should recognize that the firms adopting the emerging paradigm models do not have owner advantages to leverage. Instead, they creatively leverage *non-owner advantages* to globalise. Some firms seed some of their operations in competitive markets abroad and acquire valuable assets to fuel further growth. Others become publicly listed companies in foreign stock exchanges to secure financial resources. In some cases, they form joint ventures with non-local partners, including many in the Greater China region, to gain critical assets. Others target emerging markets (e.g., BRIC) ignored by established firms to develop a market-leading position in the sector globally.

These unorthodox strategies help the firms to overcome their weaknesses and embark on a fast learning globalisation track, allowing them to gain resources, talents, and management know-how within a short period of time. These approaches to globalisation are especially widespread among, although not limited to, firms in the banking (springboard model), technology (leapfrog model), and state-owned (mixed model) sectors.

4.2   SPRINGBOARD GLOBALISATION MODEL

4.2.1   *Characteristics of the Springboard Globalisation Model*

Contrary to the classic OLI globalisation model, the springboard model (Luo and Tung, 2007) suggests that firms can expand globally without first achieving competitive advantages in the home country. In fact, many springboard firms are latecomers to global competition. By adopting the springboard mentality, they do not focus on how competitive they are relative to other global players; rather, they focus on how much they can gain by placing themselves in a different business environment. By going abroad, they can 'bypass' home-country barriers in trade, investment, and policies, while at the same time gaining operational competences in non-local settings. In other words, the springboard model allows firms to sidestep China's institutional voids (e.g., the lack of legal protection for property rights, poor enforcement of commercial laws, weak judicial and litigation systems, underdeveloped markets, and inefficient market intermediaries) and operate in a market-driven environment conducive to developing competitive advantages.

Senior managers of these firms can secure shareholders' and investors' support by convincing them that operating in a global and free-market environment is beneficial to the firm's future. These firms often begin by experimenting with some aspects of globalisation, such as setting up an operating unit outside of mainland China (in Hong Kong or in an overseas market). If the potential gains are realised, their globalisation efforts will be strengthened.

4.2.2   Motivations to Adopt the Springboard Model

To many firms, this unconventional path is risky. Since it defies conventional management thinking, internal support to adopt the springboard strategy is often low. Nevertheless, some firms are 'forced' to take up the challenge due to intense competitive pressure in mainland China. After China joined the WTO in December 2001, a large proportion of China's restricted markets opened up to global competition. To private and foreign firms, these unrestricted markets offered exceptional opportunities, which they eagerly took up. To firms that used to 'monopolise' the formerly restricted markets, including many SOEs, their survival was being challenged. They could no longer continue their unreasonably high economic rents, leveraging low financial costs and being protected behind barriers that shut out private and foreign firms.

China's commercial banks offer good examples of the springboard model. In the midst of the WTO challenge, a senior executive of China's largest commercial bank, the Industry and Commerce Bank of China (ICBC), said, 'We are worse than candles burning at both ends.' This was indeed the case. New entrants in China offered new and competitive services to win over existing customers, thus lowering the state-owned bank's revenue. Meanwhile, ICBC and similar banks were incurring higher operational costs. They had to secure talented staff with higher salaries, pay higher rents to secure preferred branch locations, and increase advertising and promotional expenses. Further, they were losing some of their better clients, who were globalising their own businesses to meet the WTO challenge and preferred to work with banks that had global networks and related experiences. With pending revenue losses, rising costs, and defection of quality clients, commercial banks in China were forced to take a risky and unprecedented move: to expand globally without competitive advantages to leverage. This move was highly risky, but it could potentially help them gain new resources, revenue streams, and other needed assets to benefit their operations in China.

In contrast to Dunning's OLI (or the classic competitive advantage) model, aimed at leveraging the home-based ownership advantage to increase sales in the global market, China's commercial banks adopted the springboard model in the hope that going global would allow them to secure the means to save their businesses at home. Thus, they established operational units outside mainland China to gain management know-how, service innovations, and other critical assets. These resources are then transferred back to China to strengthen their positions against local counterparts. Failing to go global to gain these advantages may render them obsolete in the dynamic home market.

4.2.3 Chinese Commercial Banks Use Springboard Model to Globalise

As discussed earlier, commercial banks are the prime candidates to adopt the springboard model. Unlike manufacturing firms that adopted the OLI model to expand globally, many banks lagged behind global rivals, as their operations were 'protected' by outdated policies and institutional boundaries that have governed the banking industry in China for decades. The following paragraphs outline the characteristics of the model using China Merchant Bank (CMB) as an example.

Before 2000, the Bank of China was the only Chinese bank allowed to operate overseas. Nevertheless, CMB and other banks (e.g., ICBC) expanded to Hong Kong in the early 2000s, one year before China joined the WTO. Through their 'non-local' operations in Hong Kong, these banks learned to operate in a competitive and highly efficient financial environment to partially compensate for their disadvantages as latecomers to the global arena.

After a few years of intense learning from real-life competition in Hong Kong, CMB expanded its global operations by acquiring critical assets to become more efficient. It acquired Hong Kong's Wing Lung Bank in 2008. Its competitor ICBC acquired Hong Kong's Union Bank in 2000, as well as 80 per cent of the Bank of East Asia's American arm in 2012. These acquisitions strengthened the respective banks' strategic assets, including proprietary resources (e.g., banking licence, marketing channels), operating systems (e.g., credit card services, international operations), and management talents (international banking managers).

Through the springboard model (with forced experience learning, experimentation, and overseas acquisition), CMB gained global competence in a relatively short time. Currently, CMB's overseas and home-based operations are profitable. Their capabilities are well-respected among Chinese banks, as its stock has been trading at a relatively stable price range over the past decade. CMB also enjoys higher price–earnings ratios than other privately owned banks listed in Hong Kong (4.8 vs 4.6). Its stock price performance (which increased 13.86 per cent from 2008 to 2018) is much higher than that of global banks such as HSBC (2008–18, –37.89 per cent) and the Standard Chartered Bank (2008–18, –70.14 per cent).

In addition to commercial banks, firms in other formerly protected industries such as shipping, pharmaceuticals, and real-estate development are also exemplary candidates for the springboard model. Many of the model's adoptees are large state-owned conglomerates (e.g., Citic Group) (Luo and Tung, 2007). As SOEs or 'protected' firms, their operations have to be in line with China's industrial policies and regulations, which are likely conservative. As a result, they lag behind global and privately owned firms in the midst of the country's economic growth. However, these firms are pushed to compete, as they are losing ground in their home-based markets. In this context, the springboard model offers an innovative solution for firms to break out of their complex and institutionally confined environments.

4.2.4   Other Advantages of the Springboard Model

In addition to the previously mentioned ownership advantages, springboard firms can also secure a 'foreign' or 'non-local' status and receive preferential treatment from the Chinese government. To do so, the firm engages in 'reverse' investment; that is, they re-enter China using a 'foreign' or 'non-local' status. When Chinese firms expand globally, they are able to form legal entities and business units classified as 'non-local' or 'foreign'. The new stature associated with this move allows the firms to exploit institutional gaps and capitalise on benefits designed to attract non-local and foreign investments. If the firms are listed on the Shanghai or Shenzhen stock exchanges, their 'semi-global' identity can drive higher stock values, allowing them to enjoy lower capital costs compared to de facto local firms.

In sum, adopting the springboard model may bring three advantages to Chinese firms. First, through their non-local operations, Chinese firms have to conduct some of their businesses in open-market environments to *learn to be globally competitive*. Second, they access *resources* (talent and financial capital) otherwise unavailable to them. Third, through reverse investment, the firms may enjoy preferential treatment as a result of China's *structural gaps*. In addition, the springboard firms gain a 'globalised' image that enhances their brand image and improves staff morale. Collectively these advantages allow them to outcompete their rivals at home.

4.2.5   Implications and Challenges

While the springboard model offers obvious advantages, it also poses several challenges. When Chinese firms acquire foreign counterparts, they inevitably encounter issues with corporate integration. Integrating employees from different cultures is also a challenge. Cultural differences in management style and trust in leadership (e.g., when Lenovo acquired IBM's PC unit in 2005, many senior staff in this unit left) are critical concerns for the continuous operation of the acquired unit. Further, whether the M&A provides expected synergetic advantages depends on the management's ability to capitalise on the potential gains. If the springboard firms keep an open mindset, these issues may not be as severe.

Another challenge lies in human resources. The pool of experienced talents is limited in some sectors, such as banking. Chinese firms need to recruit and nurture talents who have an in-depth knowledge of their products and possess experiences in M&As and global operations. Their ability to manage Chinese firms with a global perspective and in a more developed regulatory environment is crucial. To compete effectively with global players, Chinese firms must step up their management development system and globalise their brand image to win market credibility.

With limited global experience, Chinese firms' strategies to springboard are often risky and aggressive. To some, the 2008 financial crisis provided a golden opportunity, as overseas assets were priced at deep discounts. This has led to a lively debate regarding whether Chinese firms vying to expand internationally should take advantage of this and other similar crises (e.g., the European economic crisis starting in 2013). Some warned that the associated risks were too high for inexperienced firms, while others opted to take advantage of the unprecedented opportunities and capitalise on the weakened global economy (Kamrany, 2011).

4.2.6   CMB: Successful Adoption of the Springboard Model

CMB is the sixth largest commercial bank by assets in China and is currently among the top 100 banks in the world. Since its founding in 1987, CMB has grown from a small bank with one overseas office to a national bank with total assets of 4.016 trillion yuan in 2013. It has more than 1,000 branches and 11,000 self-service locations across China. CMB was listed on the Shanghai Stock Exchange in 2002 and the Hong Kong Stock Exchange in 2006. It entered the American market in 2007, achieving the honour of becoming the first Chinese bank to obtain a banking licence in the USA. CMB successfully acquired Wing Lung Bank, Hong Kong's fourth largest local bank, in 2008. Valued at USD4.6 billion, it became one of the largest controlling stake acquisitions in China in 2008.

4.2.6.1   CMB's Globalisation Strategy

Set Up Stage (1986–1991) Originally a shipping company, China Merchants began to diversify its business in the mid-1980s. Its purchase of the Union Bank in 1986 represents the first acquisition of a publicly listed Hong Kong business by a Chinese firm. The following year, China Merchants set up CMB, the first commercial bank since the formation of the People's Republic of China in 1949. CMB extended its businesses into insurance and securities in 1987 and launched the subsidiary Ping An Insurance Company of China in 1988. The company also acquired existing insurance businesses in London and Hong Kong. A further extension of China Merchants' financial arm came in 1991, when it set up the securities trade group China Communications Securities.

Development Stage in the Domestic Market (1992–2002) CMB has had a representative office in Hong Kong since 1992. The representative office eventually became a branch and obtained a banking licence in Hong Kong. It was the sixth Chinese bank to receive approval from the Hong Kong Monetary Authority.

CMB identified credit cards as a major area of development to consolidate the bank's leading position in Mainland China. It pioneered and launched the 'all-in-one' card, 'all-in-one net' card, and international dual currency card. By 2006, CMB became the first Chinese bank to have issued five million cards. The dual currency card has more than 30 per cent market share, making it the largest international standard credit card in China.

Globalisation Stage (2002–Present) CMB was listed on the Shanghai Stock Exchange in 2002 and established a representative office in New York in the same year. Later, it became the first Chinese company to seek public listing in the Hong Kong Stock Exchange and was successfully listed in 2006. The offering was an immediate success; the stock price doubled after the first day of trading. CMB entered the Hang Seng China-Affiliated Corporations Index as one of the leading 'red chip' stocks of the twenty-first century.

CMB actively seek opportunities to expand overseas. It received a banking licence in the USA and opened a branch in New York in 2007, making it the first Chinese bank to do so since the USA tightened banking securities in 2001. Through its acquisition of the Wing Lung Bank in 2008, CMB expanded further in the USA and opened an offshore centre in the Cayman Islands. The acquisition allowed CMB to expand effectively overseas. In 2008–9, CMB diversified its business by investing in financial leasing, a cross-border RMB trade settlement service, and insurance capital investment outside China. Its Singapore branch, established on 22 November 2013, provides corporate customers with diversified services, including deposits, loans, trade financing, remittance, interbank funding, and forex trading. Within a month (by 31 December 2013), the branch became profitable, with a net interest income of USD303,300 and income from intermediary business of USD95,100. Figure 4.1 outlines the ranking of CMB among Fortune Global 500 companies.

4.2.6.2   *Key Success Factors*
CMB leveraged the growing domestic markets in China. It pioneered new products and continuously diversified its business. One of the company's major areas of strength is retail banking. In addition to its credit card and insurance businesses, which were discussed earlier, the company diversified into the mortgage business and real-estate agency business, targeting small- and medium-sized firms. As a result, CMB has won multiple awards for its retail banking services. It also ranks first in integrated financing ability, including its product distribution ability and the information transparency of its products. In sum, CMB has market-oriented management, entrepreneurial spirit, and a strong corporate governance structure.

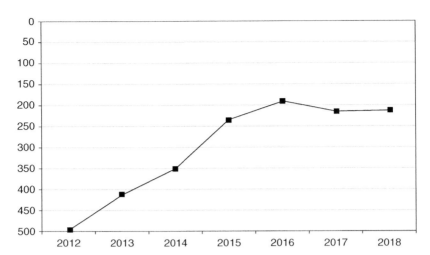

FIGURE 4.1 CMB's ranking in Fortune Global 500 list, 2012–18
Source: Fortune (2018)

4.3   LEAPFROG MODEL AND TECHNOLOGY FIRMS

The springboard model allows adoptee firms to acquire global competence and resources in a relatively short time. They may engage in non-local operations, acquire foreign assets, or become listed companies in foreign stock exchanges. These activities allow springboard firms to revise their core business model as opportunities open up.

In comparison, technology firms are more focused in their scope of business and tend to follow a predetermined strategic pattern to succeed. The following sections discuss technology firms in China, many of which adopted the leapfrog approach, a variant of the springboard model, to embark on a technological developmental path to expand globally.

4.3.1   *Characteristics of Leapfrog Technology Firms from China*

Technology firms that adopt the leapfrog model share several common characteristics. They enter high-growth industries such as telecommunication, medical equipment, alternative energy, and environmental science at times when the market has not reached saturation and is not dominated by established global firms. As a result, the Chinese newcomers are able to enter these industries with relative ease given the strong backing of local talents and encouraging government policies.

Unlike banks, which are likely to enter advanced markets to break away from regulatory constraints and to acquire valuable assets, Chinese technology firms often target developing economies that need modern, although not necessarily cutting-edge, technology. Developing economies have long been labelled by Western MNCs as 'under-developed' and weak in purchasing power. Whereas these sizeable markets house over 80 per cent of the world's population (Mahajan and Banga, 2006), established global firms ignore them, considering them unworthy of their attention. This is because most Western MNCs operate at higher cost levels, making their products and services unaffordable to developing economy markets. Further, most of these markets do not demand cutting-edge technology or top-quality product and services, thus rendering the quality or technological premium offered by global firms less critical in these markets.

In contrast, Chinese technology firms can establish themselves in these markets comfortably by offering their products/services at good price-value. Whereas technology firms are well aligned with China's national priorities, many of them are privately owned and market-driven. This gives them more flexibility to tailor their operations and strategies to meet local customer demands. In turn, the firms gain substantial global experiences and economies of scale to expand fast in a short time.

4.3.2   Science and Technology in China

With the growing recognition that technology is a primary driver of the nation's economic growth, the Chinese government pursued a long-term vision to stimulate advancement in science and technology (US–China Economic and Security Review Commission, 2005). This vision includes incentive packages at different levels of government to pool together high-tech talents (Chinese overseas specialists as returnees), financial resources (investments funds), and entrepreneurs (venture capitalists). Meanwhile, local universities nurtured a growing supply of graduates in technology-related areas. As a result, high-tech parks (e.g., Zhongguancun Science Park in Beijing, the Silicon Valley in Shenzhen) sprang up across the nation's provinces and major municipalities.

This coordinated effort, together with encouraging government policies, has given rise to many technology firms over the past decade. These include exemplary firms in the Internet (e.g., Sina, Baidu, Tencent), telecommunication (e.g., Huawei in telecom infrastructure and later communication products), and alternative energy sectors (e.g., Broad Air in air conditioning; BYD in electric cars). Although many of them later failed, as did their counterparts in the USA and Europe, some became global giants. Baidu, for example, attracted top Google executives and gradually outpaced Google to become the premier search engine in China. Baidu is now a listed company on Nasdaq. Alibaba represents another well-known success story.

Relative to commercial banks, technology firms operate in relatively market-driven conditions. However, they need access to cutting-edge technology and substantial financial resources to become globally competitive. The leapfrog approach provides these firms with a platform to obtain these critical resources. For example, Huawei invested 12.8 per cent of its sales in 2013 in research and development, and 45 per cent of its staff is involved in the firm's innovation and product development processes. In addition, it has also set up sixteen research centres in Germany, Sweden, the UK, France, Italy, Russia, India, and other countries, harvesting the host countries' technology and talents. With an ample supply of IT talents in its home base, the firm is able to continuously launch products for Chinese and international markets. Other technology firms (e.g., Baidu, Tencent, Alibaba) became publicly listed companies in overseas stock exchanges (e.g., Nasdaq, New York Stock Exchange, and Hong Kong Stock Exchange) to obtain the international stature and financial resources to fuel their growth.

Up until now, China's successful technology firms have chosen not to compete with their global rivals head-on. Most of them are content to serve the developing economies ignored by industry leaders. However, as China's economy continues to grow, operating costs will inevitably increase. Whether China's technology firms are able to maintain their cost advantage will be a critical factor for their continual success. Further, in the aftermath of the financial crisis in the American and European markets, global competition to deliver affordable technologies becomes intense. In the medical equipment field, General Electric's chairman Jeff Immelt has committed USD3 billion dollars to design affordable products for emerging economies (Immelt, Govindarajan, and Trimble, 2009). It would be unlikely for other global players such as Google or Yahoo to concede China and other emerging markets to Chinese firms. Rather, they will invest heavily, acquiring firms that possess low-cost (or affordable) innovative products, outsourcing high-cost components and redesigning cost-effective platforms to compete with their Chinese rivals.

In response, Chinese technology firms continue to innovate and move up the value chain. Serving as an indicator of this development, the number of patents granted by the Chinese patent office (2017, 2018) increased by 4.7 per cent in 2017 year-on-year. Among them, 77.8 per cent of the new patents were owned by local entities, compared to only 22.2 per cent owned by non-local entities. The local entities include Chinese firms, university centres, and individuals. With a strong national commitment, initial global success, and an ample supply of science and engineering graduates, Chinese technology firms and their globalising activities will continue to thrive.

4.3.3   Huawei: Successful Adoption of the Leapfrog Model

Founded in 1988 by Mr Ren Zhengfei, Huawei Technologies Co., Ltd is China's leading telecom solutions provider and also specialises in the development, production, and sales of telecom equipments. Based in Shenzhen with a vision to enrich life through communication, Huawei has built end-to-end integrated advantages in four business areas: telecom network infrastructure, application and software, professional services, and devices. With its strengths in wireline, wireless, and Internet protocol (IP) technologies, Huawei gained a leading position in IP convergence. As of 2013, the company employed 150,000 people and had a revenue of USD39.5 billion. The company is privately owned.

Over time, Huawei has become increasingly international. Its products and solutions have been deployed in more than 140 countries, serving forty-five of the world's fifty largest telecoms operators. Huawei has sixteen research institutes around the world. It has also established twenty-eight joint innovation centres to transform relevant leading technologies into applications.

4.3.3.1 Huawei's Globalisation Strategy

Establishing Domestic Market (1988–1999) During 1988–1999, Huawei focused on developing a strong base in the domestic market, paving the way for the company to embark on the global stage. From being a telecom equipment distributor at its founding in 1988, Huawei developed 10,000 ports (1992) and launched the C&C08 digital switch in 1994. By 1995, it engaged in a domestic expansion project by focusing first on the countryside before entering the cities – a low-cost low-risk strategy often adopted by successful domestic firms.

Internationalisation (2000–Present) Ren Zhengfei announced in 2000 that, to be an international enterprise, Huawei's earnings from the overseas market would need to surpass 50 per cent of the company's overall earnings within five years. During this period, Huawei boldly launched its global expansion plan. Rather than using Hong Kong as a stepping stone, Huawei bypassed Hong Kong and targeted developing economy markets, using the countries' telecom infrastructure as the entry point. By 2005, Huawei's overseas earnings reached 58.5 per cent of its overall earnings.

In Europe, Huawei adopted a client-focused orientation, providing a quick response, better price, and better products to the market.

The European expansion started in Russia and Eastern Europe. Experiences in these countries helped Huawei to approach other European countries and pass strict authentication procedures in order to work with British Telecom, Vodafone, France Telecom, and Telecom Italia. Huawei became the preferred supplier of British Telecom for network access and transmission services by 2005. It also signed a deal with Vodafone for its 3G handsets.

Huawei followed a similar globalisation strategy in the Americas by starting with smaller markets and second-tier carriers to build wider acceptance in the market. In September 2006, Huawei was selected by the leading telecom operator in Uruguay to construct Latin America's first Universal Mobile Telecommunications System (UMTS) network. Huawei signed a network expansion contract with Columbia Movil the same year.

Huawei has also been active in Africa's telecommunications sector, with training centres in Nigeria, Kenya, Egypt, and Tunisia to improve local technological expertise. Huawei is positioned as a low-cost, high-quality telecom provider in Africa, setting prices no more than 15 per cent below international competitors to avoid being perceived as a cheap, low-quality Chinese provider.

For Huawei, global joint ventures and alliances provide an indirect route for the company to ease market penetration. The joint venture with 3Com allowed Huawei to acquire an established name and a global network of channels in order to enter the high-end market. Huawei signed an agreement with Siemens in 2004 and established R&D centres both in China (Shenzhen, Beijing, Nanjing, Shanghai) and overseas (Sweden, the USA, Russia, India). Huawei entered a joint venture with the US-based security firm Symantec to develop security and storage solutions in 2007. The following year, it co-operated with Optus to establish a mobile innovation centre in Australia and launched a joint venture with the UK-based marine engineering company Global Marine Systems to develop undersea network equipment. Huawei has also engaged in a number of M&A activities, acquiring OptiMight in 2002 and Cognigine in 2003, and

Table 4.1 *Huawei's global footprint at a glance*

- A Fortune Global 500 company
- Second largest supplier of mobile phones
- Fifth highest investment in R&D
- Sixth largest IT company by revenue
- 170,000 employees operating in 170 countries

Source: Rauhala (2018)

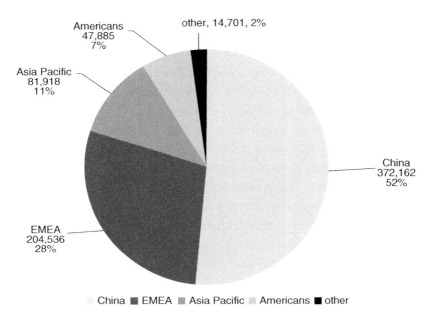

FIGURE 4.2 Huawei's revenue by region, 2018
Source: Huawei Investment and Holding Co., Ltd. (2018)

invested in LightPointe. Figure 4.2 outlines Huawei's global revenue. A summary of Huawei's global footprint can be found in Table 4.1.

Huawei is closing the gap in handsets in major markets such as France, the UK, and the USA. Huawei is currently the second handset brand by volume, with 15.8 per cent of the market in 2018 (Choudhury, 2018). Success in this market is aided by breakthroughs at the retail level, including a highly successful online promotional campaign with Amazon.com and alliances with service providers. User feedback has indicated that Huawei handsets have advantages in battery life. With such headway, the challenge for Huawei is to continue its innovation and develop additional differential advantages for the brand. Huawei has been a Fortune Global 500 firm since 2010.

4.3.3.2 Key Success Factors

There are several key success factors that account for Huawei's achievements. First, joint ventures and alliances with global giants provide a win–win strategy for partner firms. For Huawei, these ventures facilitate understanding of and entry into local markets as well as acquisition of cutting-edge technology. Second, Huawei focuses on developing markets that are largely ignored by other global players, which allows the firm to gain a competitive advantage by providing quality (although not necessarily cutting-edge) products at a *lower price*, thus providing *better value*, compared to competitors. Third, Huawei's commitment to R&D provides an advantage in its offerings. Huawei spent 14.9 per cent (or USD13.23 billion) of its 2017 revenue on R&D and it intends to raise it further to at least USD15 billion (Jiang, 2018), making it one of the top R&D spenders in the world.

In general, Chinese firms tend to have low R&D investments. With its R&D spending, Huawei has a technological edge in China. Further, 45 per cent of Huawei's employees are engaged in R&D. As a result, Huawei is well equipped with strong tech talents to compete with its global rivals.

In addition, Huawei adopts a strong service orientation and pays close attention to customer needs. The firm is quick to respond to customer demands, including on-time delivery and installation, training of local staff, and in-country support. These attributes are essential for success in the emerging markets where Huawei is heavily involved. Regarding expansion paths, Huawei started with rural market and small cities to establish a strong presence before moving to the big cities. This strategy has proven to be useful in China, and the firm has adapted it effectively in its international markets as well.

4.3.3.3   *Current Situation and Challenges*

A challenge that Huawei needs to overcome is the increasing protectionist sentiment among host countries. There have been many voices opposing Huawei's global expansion plans because of Huawei's strong market position in telecom and its presumed ties with the Chinese government. These can be seen as threats to the host nation's security. For example, Huawei's participation in building a national broadband network was blocked by the local government in Australia, its expansion in India was met with opposition, and, recently, President Trump signed a bill to ban Huawei technology from use by the US government and government contractors (Kastrenakes, 2018). These geopolitical tensions represent salient challenges for Huawei.

4.4   MIXED MODEL AND STATE-OWNED ENTERPRISES

In addition to springboarding and leapfrogging, large Chinese SOEs now engage in yet another model, a clever alternative that allows them to break out of their complex and institutionally confined environments. As SOEs, their operations are governed to a large extent by China's industrial policies and regulations. While these 'political obligations' limit the firms' operational space, they open up other possibilities. The firms may in turn leverage their favour with the government to further their positions in the industry.

As China becomes increasingly active in the highly dynamic global community, SOEs follow and benefit from China's growing global footprints. Their globalisation motive is not driven by the need to survive or to build a competitive advantage, as demonstrated by adoptees of the springboard model. Likewise, it may not concern gaining from or leveraging their technological advances, as shown by adoptees of the leapfrog model. Rather, the SOEs opt for a balance between public and for-profit concerns. Contributing to the nation's global agenda allows them to gain indirect advantages through state policies and governmental support. Their overseas operations, for example, are paid for, or at least guaranteed, by the Chinese government, so that they are faced with less financial pressure. With intensifying competition in China and in other markets, the direct (guaranteed revenue) and indirect (through policy tilts and government support) benefits extended to SOEs can be substantial. Thus, not surprisingly, there is a growing list of firms across different industries adopting the mixed model. These include construction and infrastructural firms as well as firms in the energy and transportation sectors. China's high-speed rail is an exemplar of an adoptee of the mixed model.

Driven by the country's growing urbanisation process and the need for an affordable transportation system to dramatically 'shrink' the country, China has developed its own high-speed rail system over the past decade, integrating and improving upon the technology from France, Japan, Canada, and Germany. China's high-speed rail can run at more than 350 kilometres per hour and can operate in highly difficult terrain. Its cutting-edge technology and low construction costs render it globally competitive. Using this technology, China is embarking on a path to rejuvenate the Silk Road. The proposed New Silk Road includes a main route that will start in central China, crossing Central Asia, and finally reaching Europe. Whereas the underlying political issues are beyond the scope of this book, regional and global political changes are certainly drivers for the mixed model. In the following chapters, we highlight select cases of exemplar firms to detail the practice of this emergent mixed model of globalisation.

4.5   EFFECTUAL MODEL FOR SMES

4.5.1   Effectual Model of Globalisation: China's SMEs in Africa

The previously mentioned globalisation models, including Dunning's OLI model, are appropriate for big firms. However, for China, globalisation is also practiced by thousands of SMEs that venture into the global arena to build factories and source low-cost labour to strengthen their supply chain. These SMEs do not have the financial resources, technical knowledge, or supportive policies to allow them to follow the models outlined earlier. Specifically, they do not have the size or market potential of the banks to adopt the springboard model; they do not have the technical foundation to leapfrog the technology curve; and their global moves are not supported by the Chinese government. Interestingly, while many SMEs have failed, many others have succeeded, expanding into various Asian, European, North American, and African countries. In this section, we will discuss how Chinese SMEs succeed in Africa. The reason we focus on these firms is not only that they are interesting, but also that their behaviours reflect a new model of globalisation appropriate for SMEs.

Chinese firms entered Africa as early as 1971, after twenty-six African nations voted to facilitate China's entry into the United Nations (UN). However, it is only in the last two decades that China's investments in Africa have become highly visible. According to a detailed report prepared by McKinsey (Sun, Jayaram, and Kassiri, 2017), China has become Africa's biggest economic partner in trade, investment, infrastructure financing, and aid. In McKinsey's opinion, China tops all other countries in terms of the depth and breadth of its engagement in Africa. Chinese firms of all sizes and sectors are bringing capital investment, management know-how, and entrepreneurial energy to every corner of the continent. In so doing, they help accentuate African nations' unprecedented growth.

Chinese firms operate across many sectors of the African economy. Almost 30 per cent are involved in manufacturing, 25 per cent are in services, and around 20 per cent are in trade, construction, and real estate. Sun, Jayaram, and Kassiri (2017) estimated that Chinese manufacturing firms now contribute to 12 per cent of Africa's USD500 billion annual industrial production. In infrastructure projects, Chinese firms' presence is also pronounced, winning nearly 50 per cent of Africa's international construction projects in 2015, with margins as high as 20 per cent.

4.5.2   *Chinese SMEs adopt an Entrepreneurial Mindset in Africa*

In many ways, successful SMEs behave like entrepreneurial firms. Their successes are driven by two sets of drivers. The first (and most common) set relates to the characteristics of the SMEs owners. They are hard-working, persistent, and passionate about their business. Some entered Africa with a passion, and they are bold and quick in their decisions. In one instance, an entrepreneur 'set up a polyvinyl chloride (PVC) pipe factory in a matter of weeks: "The guy just came once to Côte d'Ivoire and doesn't even speak French, but he decided immediately to go for it and invest!" Such stories are the norm rather than the exception' (Sun, Jayaram, and Kassiri, 2017, p. 33). Further, such SME owners actively work their social networks to leverage and pool all available resources. Instead of relying on bank loans, they pool financial resources personally, encouraging their friends and relatives to invest in their projects. Their quick and decisive moves allow them to out-compete many local and foreign firms.

The second set of drivers for their success is the firm strategies. Many SME owners do not have proper management training, or they choose not to use it as many of the 'learned' strategies do not apply to SMEs. Instead, the SME owners rely on a set of decision logics and heuristics postulated by the effectual theory for entrepreneurs. Specifically, they do not make decisions that go beyond the available resources and risk boundaries. Whereas a firm would usually lay out the optimal strategy, gather the resources, and then execute the set plan and maintain control to optimize the results, the effectual model puts the 'control before the optimal solution'. The SME owners thus size up the opportunity and assess whether they can afford the risk, and then they decide and act through simple heuristics. As a result, these firms are agile and quick in their decisions. While reversing the order of 'plan then control' with 'control then plan' may not provide SMEs with the maximum profit or the lowest risks, this approach has been proven effective for entrepreneurial firms in various industries.

4.5.3 *Chinese SMEs in Africa: Decision Logics and Heuristics*

Reduced Opportunity Space and Affordable Losses The effectual model recognises that SMEs are bounded by three limitations. First, given that most entrepreneurs lack experience, the ventures they engage in are highly risky. Second, most entrepreneurs have limited resources, including financial, human, and technology resources and relations in the value chain. Third, most entrepreneurs have limited market reach. This is partly because the ventures are new and partly because they do not have a recognised brand name. Thus, only a small segment of customers would consider buying products from these ventures.

These limitations are recognised by Chinese SMEs in Africa, which respond with two actions: reduced opportunity space and affordable losses. Being new and unknown in an overseas market and lacking established business relationships, the SMEs use a reduced opportunity space compared to non-SMEs and only bid for (or enter) a limited number of projects. Further, with shallow pockets, the Chinese SMEs cannot afford to lose much. As a result, they often go for 'quick kills'. After they identify projects that are doable with affordable risks, they can decide quickly. To them, the best weapon is undercutting prices. As one African government official acknowledged, the prices Chinese firms offered were usually 40 per cent lower than that of the Americans and sometimes lower than local African firms. To the Chinese entrepreneurs, the low-price entry may not bring high profits, but they are satisfied 'a bird in hand is better than two in the bush'.

Uncertain Host Environment and Little Local Support The Chinese SMEs recognise that Africa is not China, and uncertainty due to political turbulence in Africa can be high. In addition, the local banks may not be friendly providers of financial help. This 'double challenge' scenario means that they have to devise ways to manage the environmental risks with little support. They respond to these challenges in two ways.

First, they tend to enter an Africa nation in groups rather than on an individual basis. Ethiopia and South Africa have a clear strategic (and political) posture towards China. With stronger local support in investment, trade, loans, and aid, these two nations have thus attracted a large pool of Chinese entrepreneurs (e.g., networking via InterNation, 2019). In 2015, there were 60,000 Chinese expatiates in Ethiopia and 300,000–400,000 Chinese in South Africa, some of whom arrived in the early twentieth century during the nation's gold rush. Second, the Chinese entrepreneurs rely on one another when they are in need of help with either business or social matters. In Kenya, the Chinese managers and workers live on site, in housing compounds complete with a volleyball court. They rarely leave the factory precinct, even on weekends. These social bonds enable the workers to nurse their homesickness while in Africa.

Operating Along the Edge of Contingencies Another characteristic of Chinese SMEs in Africa is their ability to maximise their returns within the boundary of affordable risks. Yet, as their businesses gain traction, many of them will take up new resources and opportunities that open up. Thus, driven by strong entrepreneurship, the Chinese SMEs are consistently operating and maximising their returns as they expand their boundaries.

A typical example is that of their financial resources. More often than not, Chinese SMEs do not depend on local loans or loans offered by the Chinese government (e.g., Exxim Bank), as these loans take time and detailed documentation to process. Instead, most SMEs begin with the owners' personal resources (or those of their relatives and friends). In a McKinsey (Sun, Jayaram, and Kassiri, 2017) survey, two thirds of the private firms and more than half of all firms surveyed reported that their investments were self-financed through retained earnings or savings or were funded through personal loans. Only 13 per cent of investment funds came from financing schemes linked to the Chinese government, and less than 20 per cent came from Chinese or African commercial bank loans. Nevertheless, when the original projects paid off, the SMEs would grow or expand their businesses using the financing they could readily obtain through banking facilities.

Many of the Chinese SMEs manage the associated risks prudently. More than 50 per cent obtain their supply from overseas Chinese firms or African Chinese firms that form their familiar business network. This ensures that they will obtain a reliable supply of products (or better trade terms) than local African firms. In sum, the Chinese SMEs manage their resource-opportunity space similar to tightrope walkers on the edge of contingencies.

Exploiting Local Market Demands The fourth decision heuristic Chinese SMEs use relates to the agility (strategic flexibility) in their operations. In the manufacturing sector, few African firms have the capital, technology, and skills, and few Western firms have the risk appetite, to invest and work in these less predictable host countries. The Chinese entrepreneurs that have the skills, capital, and willingness to live there move in quickly to fill the structural gaps in the economy of the host countries. While they may begin with a limited business scope to ensure their initial success, they are not committed to a particular industry. Instead, they keep learning and expanding their businesses as they seize opportunities in the host market.

These entrepreneurs are known to be agile and quick to adapt to new opportunities. Except in a few countries such as Ethiopia, most Chinese SMEs focus on serving the needs of Africa's fast-growing markets rather than on exports. This way, they do not need to develop an export system from the African nation to other parts of the world, which can be complex and highly bureaucratic. Also, serving the local market allows them to earn returns quickly, thus reducing exchange risks and ensuring a healthy cash flow for their ventures.

4.5.4   Implications

There are more than 20,000 Chinese entrepreneurs and SMEs in African nations. They fill the structural gaps where local African firms and other foreign firms have not invested. Thus, the African people, businesses, and governments welcome these SMEs, as they help co-develop their economy and satisfy the developing nations' growing needs. Accordingly, the Chinese SMEs find the host nations welcoming, and they are optimistic about their future in Africa.

In sum, the tens of thousands of Chinese SMEs are not part of 'China Inc.', a label reserved for big Chinese firms or SOEs. Following the effectual model of entrepreneurship, their strategy and decision heuristics are new and innovative. As China embarks on its Belt and Road Initiative (BRI) in Africa, these Chinese SMEs may prove to be invaluable in their local market knowledge and business experience. For the Chinese SMEs, the BRI may offer them the needed resources and support to further elevate their presence in Africa.

4.5.5   Tecno: Products Tailored for Africa

Tecno Mobile is a highly successful Chinese SME that has followed the effectual model in its operations in African countries. The company was founded in 2006 as Tecno Telecom Limited, but it later changed its name to Transsion Holdings, with Tecno Mobile as one of its subsidiaries. During its early years, it tested the market potentials in various developing countries in South-East Asia, Africa, and Latin America, but it ultimately decided to concentrate on African countries in order to reduce the risks, even if doing so also limits the opportunities. The decision was the right one, and Tecno became one of the top three mobile phone brands in Africa in 2010. As of 2018, it has a 40 per cent market share in some East African countries, despite the presence of other global competitors. Another characteristic and

Table 4.2 *Selected Tecno smartphones and their prices in Kenya,*
2018

Devices	Price (in KSh.)	Price (in USD)	RAM/Storage
Tecno F2	6,850	66.84	1GB/8GB
Tecno Spark K7	10,399	101.46	1GB/16GB
Tecno Camon CM	14,999	146.35	2GB/16GB
Tecno Camon X Pro	23,999	234.16	4GB/64GB
Tecno Phantom 8	29,999	292.70	6GB/64GB

Source: OnlineShoppingKenya (2018)

critical success factor for Tecno is the market insight that allows it to
exploit local market demand by introducing new products specifically
tailored for this region, enabling it to outcompete other mobile companies time and again.

Tecno's devices are affordably priced (see Table 4.2) and have
features specifically tailored for African consumers. It was the first
major brand to introduce a keyboard in Amharic (Ethiopia's official
language), and it released the first 'made in Ethiopia' smartphone in
2012 to become even better embedded in the region. Tecno Mobile
then launched 'the best camera smartphone in Africa' in 2016, which
included photo software to better capture the darker skin tones of
local customers. It was recognised as the 'most student friendly
brand' in May 2017. Following its success in Ethiopia, Tecno launched
a new smartphone in Nigeria, Kenya, Ghana, South Africa, and
Uganda to build a stronger foothold in the region. In April 2018, it
launched in Nigeria the company's first phones to feature the latest
Android Operating System.

Building on its success in Africa and the company's strong
resource base, Tecno expanded to other markets to exploit opportunities there. It reaccessed some of the developing nations it had considered before, entering India in 2016 and Bangladesh and Nepal in
2017 and recently starting trial sales in Pakistan. Tecno Mobile

recognised that its strength lay in emerging markets, where the population is large but the purchasing power is low. By keeping tight control of risks, it was able to exploit a bigger market later. In sum, Tecno adopted the decision heuristics of the effectual model successfully.

4.6 CONCLUSION

4.6.1 Emerging Paradigm of Globalisation

According to Dunning's OLI normative globalisation model, firms lacking owner advantages should not expand globally. This chapter examines the experiences of some large Chinese firms (e.g., Huawei) as well as some SMEs (e.g., Tecno) that have defied conventional management thinking and embarked on their globalisation journey creatively. They experimented with alternative models, thus pointing to an emergent paradigm that complements the OLI model (see Table 4.3). As indicated in the previous discussion, the characteristics, constraints, and motivations to globalise among adoptee firms differ from one another. Springboard firms engage in globalisation to break out of the institutional void in China and develop their competitive advantages. Leapfrog firms globalise to access cutting-edge technology and resources. Mixed model firms globalise to maintain a balance between the firms' profitability and state regulations.

Meanwhile, these firms share a number of similarities that together point to the market conditions faced by Chinese firms over the past decade, after the country joined the WTO. Local firms were

Table 4.3 *Alternative models of globalisation*

Model	Prime candidates	Exemplary firms
Springboard model	Banks	CMB
Leapfrog model	Technology firms	Huawei
Mixed model	SOEs	CRRC (high-speed rail)
Effectual model	SMEs	Techno

pushed to scale a steep learning curve or risk becoming obsolete. Thus, some firms took the risky approach in spite of their lack of competitive advantages and launched their businesses in a non-local market environment. The successful firms not only survived, but outcompeted local rivals, securing new resources, talent, and management know-how not available in China.

An important segment of globalising firms is the Chinese SMEs that are proliferating to different countries and sectors. In Africa alone, there are more than 20,000 SMEs, and most of them are not factories sourcing cheap labour. Rather, they actively seek out the growing needs of the local market and fulfil such needs by producing the products locally. Many of them behave as entrepreneurs in managing their businesses, keeping a tight control on risks before maximising their opportunities. Their strategy in fulfilling local demand and their ability to balance risks and returns earns them respect from the local government and business partners.

4.6.2   Challenges Ahead

As China's economy continues to grow, it is inevitable that its cost advantages will shrink. Meanwhile, heavy investments by leading global firms targeted at emerging economy markets, as well as protectionist sentiments in some host countries, place new demands on Chinese firms. Already, some Chinese firms have moved their manufacturing base to countries with lower costs, such as South Africa, Vietnam, and North Korea. Other firms are increasing their investment in patents and R&D to seek a technological edge and move up the value chain. Yet some are seeking marketing and brand-building expertise to increase their profit margin. For the Chinese SMEs that are globalising quickly, their unique firm strategies have proven to be highly successful and will likely provide new insights on firm globalisation.

These approaches represent Chinese firms' continual development in their globalisation efforts. Given the creative approaches they have developed over the past decade of globalisation, it is expected that they will meet future challenges creatively. However, many of the challenges have not been fully revealed. These challenges will be discussed in detail in the following chapters.

REFERENCES

Chinese Patent Office. (2017). Patent annual report 2016. Retrieved 10 July 2019. www.sipo.gov.cn/docs/20180226104343714200.pdf.

Chinese Patent Office. (2018). Chinese patent statistics report 2017. Retrieved 10 July 2019. www.sipo.gov.cn/docs/20180411102303821791.pdf.

Choudhury, S. R. (2018). China's Huawei pulls ahead of Apple to become number-two smartphone seller in the world. *CNBC*. 31 July. Retrieved 10 July 2019. www.cnbc.com/2018/08/01/huawei-beats-apple-to-become-number-two-smartphone-seller.html.

Fortune. (2018). Global 500. *Fortune*. Retrieved 2 July 2019. http://fortune.com/global500/list/.

Huawei Investment and Holding Co., Ltd. (2018). 2018 Annual Report. Retrieved 10 July 2019. www-file.huawei.com/-/media/corporate/pdf/annual-report/annual_report2018_en.pdf?la=zh.

Immelt, J. R., Govindarajan, V., and Trimble, C. (2009). How GE is disrupting itself? *Harvard Business Review*, 87(10): 56–65.

InterNation. (2019). Retrieved 11 July 2019. www.internations.org/ethiopia-expats/chinese.

Jiang, S. (2018). China's Huawei to raise annual R&D budget to at least $15 billion. *Reuters*. 26 July. Retrieved 10 July 2019. www.reuters.com/article/us-huawei-r-d/chinas-huawei-to-raise-annual-rd-budget-to-at-least-15-billion-idUSKBN1KG169.

Kamrany, N. M. (2011). China's rapid recovery in the Great Recession of 2007–2009. *Huffpost*. 25 May. Retrieved 10 July 2019. www.huffingtonpost.com/nake-m-kamrany/chinas-rapid-recovery-in-_b_825194.html.

Kastrenakes, J. (2018). Trump signs bill banning government use of Huawei and ZTE tech. *The Verge*. 13 August. Retrieved 10 July 2019. www.theverge.com/2018/8/13/17686310/huawei-zte-us-government-contractor-ban-trump.

Luo, Y. D. and Tung, L. (2007). International expansion of emerging market enterprises: a springboard perspective. *Journal of International Business Studies*, 38(4): 481–98.

Mahajan, V. and Banga, K. (2006). *The 86 Percent Solution: How to Succeed in the Biggest Market Opportunity of the Next 50 Years*. Upper Saddle River, NJ: Pearson Education.

OnlineShoppingKenya. (2018). Retrieved 8 December 2018. https://onlineshoppingkenya.com/tecno-phones-pricelist.

Rauhala, E. (2018). What to know about China's Huawei technologies. *Washington Post*. 6 December. Retrieved 10 July 2019. www.washingtonpost.com/world/2018/12/06/what-know-about-chinas-huawei-technologies/?noredirect=on&utm_term=.7dcd0075a6c4.

Sun, I. Y., Jayaram, K., and Kassiri, O. (2017). *Dance of the Lions and Dragons: How Are Africa and China Engaging, and How Will the Partnership Evolve?* New York: McKinsey Global Institute.

US–China Economic and Security Review Commission. (2005). 2005 Annual Report to Congress. Retrieved 23 July 2019. www.uscc.gov/Annual_Reports/2005-annual-report-congress.

5   Challenges and Failures

5.1 INTRODUCTION

The path for Chinese firms to go global has not been getting any easier over time. During the early years of their globalisation efforts, the firms' goals were simple and straightforward. The challenges at that time were mostly internal and management-oriented. Using an export mode of operation, the firms were driven by the need to produce products with reasonable quality and then export them at low prices. Challenges related to this value-based approach to exporting include finding the right distributors for market entry and sustaining sales in these overseas markets. Nevertheless, there were a few factors that hampered firms' export efforts, leading to failures. They include the firms' inexperience in exporting, the lack of loan facilities (few commercial banks provide export loans) and inefficient government export systems to provide adequate support to firm export activities. As these failed exports were small and lacked public interests, most of them did not appear in the mass media.

As time went by and Chinese firms expanded their globalisation objectives, the challenges intensified and became more varied. The new challenges often went beyond the firms' internal management and included accusations on how their overseas operations were mismanaged. Some of the firms' globalisation plans, such as major M&As, were elevated to security concerns in host countries and, at times, became the bases for international disputes. These instances were highlighted in the media, and the Chinese firms were frequently portrayed as culprits. Not surprisingly, the public image of Chinese firms suffered in the world market. By December 2013, these challenges intensified, and various parties in the USA published high-profile reports and task force studies (e.g., Princeton Task Force on Chinese Investment in the United States, 2013) that raised concerns on the globalisation of Chinese firms. Currently, various governments and policy-related institutions, especially in the USA (Heritage Foundation, Rodiumy Group, and China-US Focus site) are monitoring the globalisation of Chinese firms.

5.1.1　Challenges in Early Globalisation Were Mostly Learning-Related

We pointed out in Chapter 2 that the global economic community was excited when China opened its doors in 1979. During this 'honeymoon' period before China's ascension to the WTO, the sentiments were positive. Many regarded China as an Asian economy relying on low-cost exports to propel its economic growth. Many MNCs invested and built their production facilities in China, with American and Japanese firms leading the way. By law, foreign investors had to form joint ventures with Chinese firms to operate in the country. This global rush has led to a robust growth of factories that first appeared in southern China and later expanded to the Zhejiang (near Shanghai) and Yangzi River Delta, which produced commodity-type products (household goods and personal items) to meet the world's high demand for these goods. The joint-venture firms fuelled the growth of factories and were instrumental in transferring related technologies to China.

By 1998, China's exports surpassed those of Korea; six years later in 2004, China's exports surpassed those of Japan, making China Asia's top exporting country and third in the world (behind Germany and the USA). During these twenty-five years of growth (1979–2004), many global firms empathised with China and gladly supported the country's development and economic reform. To facilitate the function and efficiency of this production hub, they helped build highly efficient supply chains and elevated China to become the single most important global production base in the world. Production management talents and the needed technology also poured in, transforming

China into the world's factory. Nevertheless, most of China's exports during this period were either low-price commodity products or OEM for global brands. In turn, Chinese SOEs, including Haier, successfully built upon the technologies transferred during this period and began their own paths to globalisation. Figure 5.1 outlines China's exports during this period when compared to that of other economies.

5.1.2   Challenges to Exports: Internal and Management-Oriented

During this early phase of globalisation, the firms' goals were simple and straightforward. Accordingly, the challenges were mostly internal, including issues in production (maintaining quality and product safety standards), trade (certification and financing of export trade), and marketing (finding distributors and wholesalers in host markets). Meanwhile, the firms' lack of experience in global operations was reflected in their overconfidence, insensitivity to the host country's culture, and inability to find the right distributors. The exports during this period included agricultural products, handicrafts, and small tools. Manufacturers for household appliances (such as TCL) and cars (Chery) were good examples of firms during this era.

5.1.3   WTO: A Turning Point of Global Sentiments

China's ascension to the WTO in 2001 became both a favourable and an unfavourable factor in Chinese firms' globalisation efforts. On the one hand, it opened up China to the world economy, with global MNCs pouring in to stimulate the country's economy. It also forced Chinese firms to learn and approach world manufacturing standards, as they were required to follow the WTO's framework agreement. However, ascension to the WTO also triggered the global community to look at China as a potential economic world power and thus a threat. Increasingly, global consumers and host governments expect Chinese firms to attain higher standards in their products and operations. Accordingly, tolerance towards China and lower-quality products produced there began to decrease. Thus, ascension to the WTO

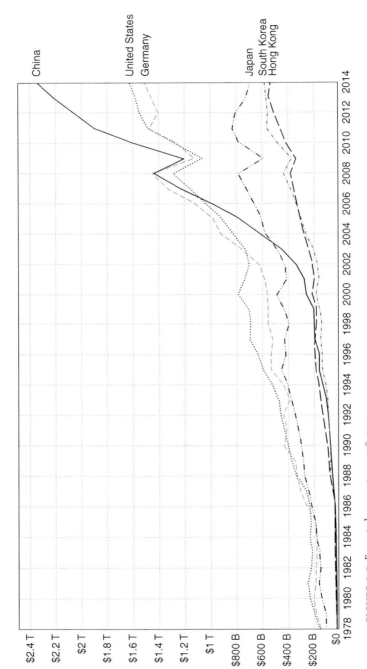

FIGURE 5.1 Exports by country, 1978–2014
Source: World Trade Organization (2018)

serves as a milestone marking the globalisation of both the Chinese economy and the firms therein, with long-term consequences.

This fundamental change in the global community's attitude towards China and its firms was partly driven by the changing motives of Chinese firms. As they evolved from an export-only mode to operations that also involve FDIs, their globalisation models became complex, resulting in new challenges. These, together with the rising expectations from consumers and host governments around the world, gave rise to new concerns and failures.

Between 2004 and 2011, Chinese SOEs suffered from eleven cases of major losses in their global operations (Table 5.1). These cases cut across industries and firm types and were geographically dispersed, including failures in Asia, Europe, Australia, and beyond.

Table 5.2 lists the types of mistakes that Chinese firms made during this period, including the globalisation modes used and notable examples.

5.2   TYPES OF MISTAKES MADE BY CHINESE FIRMS

5.2.1   *Challenges in Exporting: Product Safety*

During the mid-1980s, MNCs such as Nike began to move their production units to China, driven by the intensifying global price competition. The move sparked the development of highly cost-efficient value chains that empowered China to gain its world-factory status. With its cost advantages and world-factory status, China gradually sucked out production units first from Chinese Taiwan and Hong Kong, and then from other Asian economies, Europe and North America. This in turn intensified global price competition and led to the growth of mega distributors such as Walmart and Carrefour.

In the midst of these developments, a major issue involving Chinese-made products surfaced: that of product safety that included auto tyres (Welch, 2007) and lead-painted toys (Lipton and Barboza, 2007). In 2007, close to 80 per cent of Chinese-made toys exported to the USA were recalled. These were followed by recalls of tainted milk

Table 5.1 *Major losses incurred by Chinese firms between 2004 and 2011*

Year	Country	Company	Loss	Reason
2004	France	TCL	Recourse by creditors for €23.1 million (~RMB211 million)	Misjudged the developmental trend of the industry
2004	Singapore	China National Aviation Fuel Group (CNAF)	Loss of USD550 million due to oil derivatives trading	Failed in derivative investment
2004	China	China National Cotton Reserves Corporation (CNCRC)	Gambling on the price increase in cotton and lost about RMB1 billion at the end of 2004	Failed in futures investment
2005	Korea	SAIC Motor	Paid RMB4.1 billion on acquiring nearly 50 per cent of the shares of South Korea's SsangYong Motor, and then SsangYong filed for bankruptcy reorganisation	Market fluctuation caused by financial crisis and cultural differences
2008	Belgium	Ping An Insurance	Providing a total of RMB22.79 billion for huge losses	Financial crisis
2008	Australia	CITIC Limited	Leveraged foreign exchange contracts for iron ore and lost more than HKD10 billion	Failed in options investment
2008	China	China Eastern Airlines	Aviation oil hedging loss of RMB6.2 billion	Failed in futures investment

Year	Country	Company	Description	
2008	China	China Ocean Shipping (Group) Company (COSCO)	Carrying out forward freight agreement hedging, which led to a loss of RMB4.121 billion at the end of 2008	Failed in futures investment
2010	Saudi Arabia	China Railway Construction Corporation (CRCC)	Saudi Arabia's light rail project had a loss of RMB4.2 billion, which is paid by the state	Signed the contract hastily
2011	The Netherlands	China Overseas Holdings Limited (COHL)	Completion on time would result in a loss of USD394 million. After the project was stopped, the Dutch owner recovered USD271 million in compensation	Signed the contract hastily
2011	Australia	Sinosteel	RMB10 billion investment in midwestern Australia, has suspended development	Insufficient investment risk estimate

Source: Caixin.com (2011)

Table 5.2 *Globalisation mode, types of mistakes, and notable examples*

Globalisation mode	Types of mistakes	Notable examples
Export	Product safety	Toys, auto tyres, food
Export	Market sustainability	3 per cent rule, low conversion
Export	Insensitive to host-market firms	Shoe export to Spain
Financial – Energy hedging	Risk management	Oil pricing and Asian financial crisis
Financial – Public listing	Lack of listing planning	Privatise and move back to Hong Kong/China
Infrastructure	Contract honouring	Poland A2 highway
Local operations	Labour law	In Africa: working environment, lack of upward mobility
Mining operations	Environmental concern	Mining in Africa
Resource acquisition	Corruptive action	Rio Tinto
M&As – Food	Strategic resources	Largest food processing in USA
M&As – Real estate	Inflationary pressure	Housing purchase

in 2008 and 2014 (Huang, 2014) and other foods and beverages in 2009 (Gale and Buzby, 2009). As a result of these issues, Chinese-made products have been stigmatised internationally with a highly unfavourable image.

While a small portion of hazardous products came from unethical firms or farms, the major instances came from MNCs (e.g., Mattel toys) and large Chinese firms (e.g., Mengnui Dairy products). In short, these product hazards can and should be avoided, given these firms' resources and expected quality control standards. Whereas similar instances have since decreased, some highly publicised cases (e.g., Chinese-made hover boards that caught fire in 2015) continuously reinforce the stereotype of poor-quality Chinese-made products.

5.2.2 Inability to Gain Sustainable Market Presence in Host Markets

Chinese firms are highly price competitive. Given their low production costs, they can price their products aggressively in export markets. This was indeed the case when they entered the Spanish shoe market, where they adopted predatory pricing in the hope of quickly sustaining their market shares. In response, local merchants held a strong and violent protest. On 16 September 2004, a Chinese-owned shoe warehouse was burnt down in Elche, Spain, causing damage totalling more than €1 million. The Spanish manufacturers and distributors worried that such pricing tactics would not only erode their market shares, but ultimately destroy their industry (Adler, 2004)

Even with their low prices, most Chinese firms fail to gain sufficient market shares to sustain their presence in some host markets, especially in the USA. In developed markets, a firm needs a 4 per cent share to sustain its operations (i.e., to earn sufficient revenue to pay for the advertising, promotion, selling, and distribution). Being new to the global market and hampered by weak brand awareness and low channel penetration, many Chinese firms fail to gain and maintain this sustainable share level. Thus, many withdraw from the host market after a few years.

Other firms suffer from a similar fate when they sell their products to large distributors such as Walmart or Costco. As many Chinese firms have low brand awareness, they do not have the brand power to bargain with these large discounters. As a result, their entry into North American or West European markets is extremely challenging. Partly for this reason, the majority of Chinese firms turn to developing countries, where consumers are attracted by the products' good price-value.

5.3   FAILURES IN MINING AND RESOURCES INDUSTRIES

5.3.1   *Failures in Managing Workforce in Mining Operations*

Chinese mining and resource-based firms face different types of challenges as they globalise their operations. Specifically, failure in managing the local labour force is a critical factor in many Chinese resource ventures in Africa. The following are some notable instances.

In November 2011, a major labour dispute erupted in a copper mine in Zambia, the largest mining operation in which a Chinese firm, China Non-Ferrous Metals Mining Corporation (CNMC), was involved. More than 1,000 miners went on strike. There were two prominent issues. First, many miners complained that each week they were working five twelve-hour shifts as well as a sixth eighteen-hour 'change shift' when they rotated from the day shift to the night shift or vice versa. Other miners complained that they worked 365 days without a single day off.

Further, there were issues of safety. Miners complained that the firm focused only on productivity and was unconcerned with labour safety. As one miner on strike described,

> We are working in very bad conditions, horrible conditions. After a blast, it takes an hour for the dust, gases and fumes to clear the area. We're supposed to wait but with the Chinese, they say, 'Go, go, rush in right away!' And if you don't, they'll terminate your contract. So we go straight into an area full of fumes and dust ... The doctor said that these gases have caused my ulcers and chest pain.

Under pressure from the Zambian government, the firm reinstated the miners it had terminated. It also changed its labour contract supplier and improved its poor labour practices (Chen and Han, 2011).

Increasingly, host-country governments are demanding that Chinese firms engage local staff at higher-level jobs, such as engineers, in their operations. They see this as an opportunity to reduce the resistance to their efforts to bring in Chinese firms that might be seen as exploiting local low-cost labour. Such challenges are not only increasing in mining operations, but also spreading to industries such as telecommunication infrastructure. Huawei, for example, has designed and publicised new training programmes in Africa to reduce these pressures (ChinaFile, 2016), yet the company has been lax in reporting the effectiveness of these programmes. It remains to be seen if the skills learned can be applied beyond Huawei so that young locals can work in other companies in the IT industry.

5.3.2 Inexperience in Negotiating Mining and Resource Deals

A more serious challenge to Chinese firms lies in corrupt prac-tices. In July 2009, Chinese steel mills (including Shougang Group and Laigang Group) were negotiating with Rio Tinto, a British-Australian MNC and one of the world's largest metal and mining corporations about the future prices of steel. Later, Rio Tinto's lead negotiator Stern Hu (together with four other staff) were charged with espionage (for obtaining confidential information on Chinese firms) and bribery (accepting about USD900,000) in trying to settle a price for China to buy iron ore from Australian mining companies. Hu admitted the charges and was subsequently sen-tenced to jail.

Some attributed this instance partly to Rio Tinto's refusal to sell part of the company to the Chinese state-owned company Chinalco. Subsequently, a survey of American businesses, released at the Rio Tinto trial, showed that one third of them indicated that, under the Chinese legal and regulatory system, they were discriminated against when compared to their Chinese rivals (BBC News, 2010). Similar corruption charges were made against Chinese firms in their involvement in Africa's largest iron-ore mining project (Economist, 2014).

These cases suggest that Chinese firms are inexperienced in handling confidential information in major commodity negotiations. The current practice not only damages trading partners, but also projects negative images of Chinese firms.

5.4   FAILURES IN INFRASTRUCTURE DEVELOPMENT

5.4.1   *Failures in Obtaining and Honouring Contracts in Infrastructure Development*

Chinese firms have been highly competitive in building infrastructure in overseas markets. Their ability to deliver quality work at low costs is especially welcomed by developing countries. Nevertheless, these firms face challenges in their overseas operations. In 2009, three Chinese firms (including Overseas Chinese Construction) won a contract to jointly construct a 49-kilometre highway in Poland to prepare for the European football championship in 2012. However, they were not able to finance the project once the construction was underway and thus were unable to continue with the project. In subsequent negotiation, the contract was withdrawn. This project was previously heralded in the Chinese press as an exemplary project to open up the infrastructure market in Europe. Unfortunately, it became a high-profile failure due to inadequate financial planning. The failure of this project revealed two major issues in Chinese firms' going-out efforts. In addition to the inexperience of the infrastructure firms that had to take the ultimate responsibility for this failure, the lack of support from Chinese banks and related government units also contributed to these failures.

Another notable failure, as reported in the *Financial Times* in February 2017, was that the Beijing-funded 350-kilometre Belgrade–Budapest link, which was intended to connect the capitals of Serbia and Hungary, might have violated EU laws, which stipulate that public tenders must be used for large transport projects. As such, this project did not meet all the legal requirements (Financial Times, 2017a). This high-profile project was part of China's USD900 billion BRI to win diplomatic friends in Europe, Asia, and Africa. Thus, the failure to comply with regional laws may have negative repercussions for China's BRI.

5.4.2 Failures in Gaining Local Supports in Infrastructure Development

Infrastructure projects are megaprojects that inevitably need strong local supports to succeed. This has been a major challenge to the Asian expansion of the high-speed rail system, which cuts across seven Asian countries including Laos, Vietnam, Thailand, Myanmar, Cambodia, Malaysia, and Singapore. As part of China's BRI in Asia, this high-speed rail system forms a Pan-Asia railway network. The project's success anchors on a series of skilful bilateral negotiations that involve national priorities, developmental strategies, and efforts to gain support across villages and small towns in the northern Asian forest (Kratz and Pavlićevi, 2017).

While some progress has been made, this project has been challenged by villages and communities that were not involved in the negotiation. In 2016, some breakthroughs were reported (Martin, 2016), but the controversy will likely continue. Thus, the Chinese high-speed rail firms need to work hard both at the government level and the local village level.

Take for example the Mekong rail project. To date, the negotiation concerning the 873-kilometre Sino–Thai railway (as part of the 4,500-kilometre system) has failed to resolve some major differences, including how the project would be funded and the conditions of the loans. While the project is recognised as a crucial plank in the efforts to build a transport and trade bridge between China and the South-East Asian region that houses more than 600 million people, negotiations often break down as opponents bring up issues in the economic, environmental, and regional domains. The Laos route of the system as proposed would be under the control of Chinese firms, which would likely raise sovereignty and national security concerns.

5.5   FAILURES IN M&AS

5.5.1   *Global M&As: Host-Country National Security Concerns*

Chinese firms have adopted M&As as another globalisation strategy. As indicated in Chapter 2 of this book, Chinese FDIs in the USA grew thirteen-fold between 2005 and 2016 to reach USD53.9 billion in 2016. Accordingly, some businesses are labelling this exponential growth phenomenon as 'owned by China', to differentiate it from the previous era of 'made in China' (Princeton Task Force on Chinese Investment in the United States, 2013). Globally, Chinese FDIs ranked the third highest in the world in 2017, just behind the USA and Japan (United Nations Conference on Trade and Development, 2018).

Whereas conventional wisdom welcomes FDI as a boost to the host economy, the growth of China's FDI was perceived differently. In Africa, Europe, and, in particular, the USA, many people are raising concerns over these Chinese investments, with the top concern being national security. For example, the FDI of two telecom giants, Huawei and ZTE, drew the attention of some US policymakers, as these firms were perceived as having a strong relationship with the Chinese government. The US policymakers pointed out that if these firms were to become involved in US telecommunication infrastructure projects, there would be risks of spying and cyberattacks. As a result, they set up a Permanent Select Committee on Intelligence and Committee on Foreign Investment in the United States to help regulate the extent of Huawei's and ZTE's operations in the USA (Harwit, 2016).

Another example occurred in the oil refinery industry in 2012. In this case, Chinese firms such as Sany and Cnooc attempted to invest in locations close to US military facilities. Their actions raised concerns related to potential involvement of the Chinese government (Penty and Forden, 2013). More recently, when Shuanghui attempted in 2013 to buy Smithfield Foods, a large meat-processing company that has facilities in twenty-six states and handles 87 per cent of all pork sold in the USA, the M&A was perceived as a potential national security issue by some who advocated that food is a strategic resource and should be regulated (PBS News Hour, 2014).

While no one can be entirely certain of the motives behind these (and other similar) acquisitions, the fact is that the focal Chinese firms were insensitive to how their M&A activities may be perceived by the public and policymakers of the host country. This insensitivity with regard to their own actions demonstrates the extent of Chinese firms' lack of global experience. If they approach M&A situations with higher sensitivity, the outcomes may unfold differently. Alternatively, they could employ global consulting firms experienced in these areas in order to be more sensitive in dealing with host-country issues.

5.5.2   Global M&As: Doubts of Acquisition Motives

M&As by Chinese SOEs often involve large investments. This is partly because China's state government is an influential (if not the majority) shareholder in SOEs. As a result, stakeholders in host countries tend to scrutinise these M&As and closely monitor the potential consequences of the deals. Also, whistle-blowers have raised various issues and concerns. Increasingly, similar doubts have spread to M&As by privately owned Chinese firms. The challenges are related not to national security concerns, but to the loss of local firms' competitiveness in the long run. In particular, two types of proprietary assets are of concern.

First, host-country firms become concerned when Chinese firms buy their brand names, especially those with a national reputation. Chinese firms have a short corporate history, and most of them do not have the talent to build strong brands. As a result, many Chinese firms prefer to buy brands with global stature in order to establish their names quickly in the global economy. The earliest major purchase of this type was Lenovo's acquisition of IBM's laptop (and desktop computer) business in 2004. More recently, in

January 2017, McDonald's sold the majority stake of its China business to the Citic Group. These high-profile purchases highlighted the economic power of private firms in China. However, these purchases cause people in the host countries to speculate the extent the cash-rich Chinese firms would affect their lives as they continue to acquire firms with high market shares. In 2016, Chinese firms invested USD42.1 billion (representing a 360 per cent surge from USD11.7 billion in 2015) in the USA. Moreover, they comprised 12 per cent of all inbound M&As in the USA that year, compared to just 2 per cent the previous year (Financial Times, 2017b).

The same situation can be seen in Europe. Chinese companies are welcomed, as they provide fresh capital for ailing European enterprises. These include the Swedish carmaker Volvo (acquired by Geely in 2010), the Italian tyre maker Pirelli, the French resort operator Club Med, and the port in Piraeus, Greece. In 2016, these purchases reached €20 billion, or USD22.4 billion, according to a survey by Rhodium Group and the Mercator Institute.

In more recent cases, M&A activities have spread to companies with crucial technologies. While the purchases are welcome, there are concerns over the motives of the Chinese firms. Some doubt if the Chinese firms will continue to support R&D investments in these firms. They fear that the Chinese firms will exploit the technology and use it in the Chinese market without additional development. Should this happen, employment and talent development in the acquired firms will suffer.

Another concern that has been raised is the loss of long-term competitiveness. This is the case regarding China's Midea Group (one of the top three appliance manufacturers in China), which owns 95 per cent of the shares of Kuka, a well-known robotics company whose technology is ubiquitous in German car factories. Increasingly, people in Germany are concerned whether the core technology of Kuka may be transferred to China's car industry. If this happens, the German auto industry may suffer. Similar issues have been raised as

Chinese firms have attempted to acquire electronic chip companies in the USA.

One may argue that these concerns are driven by the narrow-mindedness of the global community and its failure to adjust its perceptions towards Chinese firms. Nonetheless, these unfavourable perceptions are salient, and, unless Chinese firms are more transparent and become better known to the world, their unfavourable image will likely continue. In subsequent chapters, we shall discuss how Chinese firms and the Chinese government deal with these perception issues.

5.5.3 Conclusion

The globalisation of Chinese firms is now an accepted trend in the global economy, yet few would have predicted the pace at which Chinese firms have embraced globalisation and the variety of globalisation models they have adopted. On a rational level, it is natural that fast-expanding and cash-rich Chinese firms would globalise their operations, as this move would provide the firms with new markets and financial capital. At a global level, the move could benefit the ailing world economy. Given their lower entry barriers, developing economies are highly attractive to the investing Chinese firms. Such investments are especially welcome by developing economies, given the persistent and widening wealth gap between rich and poor nations.

Nevertheless, Chinese firms' globalisation move has raised many eyebrows. Indeed, many firms have experienced difficulties and failures in their globalisation efforts. First and foremost, the firms' lax product safety control mechanisms and human resource management do not meet global standards. The poor product safety record cuts across different industries and has brought widespread product recalls in selected industries (e.g., toys). This perception of poor quality has unfortunately spread to include most 'made in China' products, making image perception an important issue if Chinese firms are to succeed in overseas markets.

In addition, the firms' inexperience in the global arena plays a key part in some firm failures. Their partners in international negotiation are often the host-country governments, and their strong reliance on government-level negotiations is highly risky as host-country governments change hands. This approach to negotiation also begs enquiries into corruption concerns if the process is not transparent. In the worst-case scenario, it could lead to corruption charges against the investing firms.

Relatedly, Chinese firms using M&As to enter the host country need to become responsible corporate citizens engaged in local communities. Engagement with host-country stakeholders, including the media and consumers, could help reduce the negativity towards Chinese firms. This is especially needed in countries that are concerned with China and its firms' growing dominance in the global economy. In summary, Chinese firms need, first and foremost, to improve their internal management processes to succeed in the overseas market. In the meantime, the perceptions they project, either individually as a specific firm or collectively as Chinese firms as a whole, would play an increasingly important part in host-country acceptance of their operations. In Part II of this book, we will turn to examine Chinese firms' image as well as China's image in overseas markets and their implications regarding Chinese firms' going-global efforts.

REFERENCES

Adler, K. (2004). Spanish fury over Chinese shoes. *BBC News*. 24 September. Retrieved 12 July 2019. http://news.bbc.co.uk/2/hi/europe/3687602.stm.

BBC News. (2010). Rio Tinto executives 'admit bribery' at China trial. *BBC News*. 22 March. Retrieved 12 July 2019. http://news.bbc.co.uk/2/hi/asia-pacific/8579276.stm.

Caixin.com. (2011). 中国企业海外巨亏案例一览 (Chinese firms' major overseas blunders, an overview). *Caixin*. 25 July. Retrieved 12 July 2019. http://photos.caixin.com/2011-07-25/100283356.html.

Chen, H. and Han, W. (2011). China-Zambia strike event. *Caixin*. 5 November. Retrieved 12 July 2019. http://topics.caixin.com/2011-11-05/100322836_all.html.

ChinaFile. (2016). Is Huawei doing enough to train local staff in Africa? *ChinaFile*. 23 August. Retrieved 12 July 2019. www.chinafile.com/china-africa-project/huawei-doing-enough-train-local-staff-africa.

Economist. (2014). Crying foul in Guinea. *The Economist*. 4 December. Retrieved 12 July 2019. www.economist.com/news/business/21635522-africas-largest-iron-ore-mining-project-has-been-bedevilled-dust-ups-and-delays-crying-foul.

Financial Times. (2017a). EU sets collision course with China over 'silk road' rail project. *Financial Times*. 19 February. Retrieved 12 July 2019. www.ft.com/content/003bad14-f52f-11e6-95ee-f14e55513608.

Financial Times. (2017b). Surge in Chinese corporate investment into the US. *Financial Times*. 1 January. Retrieved 12 July 2019. www.ft.com/content/b0cc57c8-d09f-11e6-9341-7393bb2e1b51.

Gale, F. and Buzby, J. C. (2009). Imports from China and food safety issues. Economic Information Bulletin no. 52, July. US Department of Agriculture, Economic Research Service.

Harwit, E. (2016). Sanctioning ZTE and Huawei: Chinese telecom giants' conflicts with the U.S. China-US Focus. *China-US Focus*. 30 June. Retrieved 12 July 2019. www.chinausfocus.com/finance-economy/sanctioning-zte-and-huawei-chinese-telecom-giants-conflicts-with-the-u-s.

Huang, Y. (2014). The 2008 milk scandal revisited. *Forbes*. 16 July. Retrieved 12 July 2019. www.forbes.com/sites/yanzhonghuang/2014/07/16/the-2008-milk-scandal-revisited/#f4dc69f44282.

Kratz, A. and Pavlićevi, D. (2017). Chinese high-speed rail in Southeast Asia: fast-tracking China's regional rise? *Reconnecting Asia*. 18 September. Retrieved 12 July 2019. https://reconnectingasia.csis.org/analysis/entries/chinese-high-speed-rail-southeast-asia/.

Lipton, E. S. and Barboza, D. (2007). As more toys are recalled, trail ends in China. *New York Times*. 19 June. Retrieved 12 July 2019. www.nytimes.com/2007/06/19/business/worldbusiness/19toys.html?_r=0.

Martin, N. (2016). China's high-speed rail plans for Asia inch closer. *Deutsche Welle*. 27 April. Retrieved 12 July 2019. www.dw.com/en/chinas-high-speed-rail-plans-for-asia-inch-closer/a-19217479.

PBS News Hour. (2014). Who's behind the Chinese takeover of world's biggest pork producer? *PBS News Hour*. 12 September. Retrieved 12 July 2019. www.pbs.org/newshour/show/whos-behind-chinese-takeover-worlds-biggest-pork-producer.

Penty, R. and Forden, S. (2013). Cnooc said to cede control of Nexen's U.S. gulf assets. *Bloomberg*. 2 March. Retrieved 12 July 2019. www.bloomberg.com/news/articles/2013-03-01/cnooc-said-to-cede-control-of-nexen-s-u-s-gulf-assets.

Princeton Task Force on Chinese Investment in the United States. (2013). Responding to Chinese direct investment in the United States. *Princeton University*. 6 December. Retrieved 12 July 2019. https://scholar.princeton.edu /sites/default/files/smeunier/files/Owned%20by%20China%20Class%20Rep ort.pdf.

United Nations Conference on Trade and Development. (2018). *World Investment Report 2018*. New York: United Nations.

Welch, D. (2007). Made in China: faulty tires. *Bloomberg News*. 12 July. Retrieve 12 July 2019. www.bloomberg.com/news/articles/2007-07-12/made-in-china-faulty-tiresbusinessweek-business-news-stock-market-and-financial-advice.

World Trade Organization. (2018). International trade statistics, electronic dataset. Retrieved 12 July 2019. http://data.wto.org/.

6 Product Images and Market Acceptance of Chinese-Made Products

6.1 INTRODUCTION

The previous chapter discussed the market challenges faced by Chinese firms and how some of them failed as they globalised or acquired firms (including factories, brands, and technology) in the global market. The current chapter centres on another major challenge faced by Chinese firms: achieving consumer acceptance in economically developed markets. It begins with a discussion on how consumers from different countries perceive China and its products. It pays attention to the unfavourable made-in-China image, a powerful bias known to twist consumers' objective product quality and safety evaluations. Often, this bias has motivational roots traceable to perceived animosity towards China and ethnocentrism (in this context, a need to defend a person's home economy against Chinese imported products). This motivational bias further suppresses consumer intentions to buy Chinese brands and products. However, emerging studies uncover that culturally open and world-minded consumers are less susceptible to these biases, pointing to ways that this stereotype against Chinese brands and products is being revised. The chapter also discusses the success of some Chinese firms and their favourable spillovers on perceptions of Chinese firms and their products.

6.1.1 China's National and Made-in-China Image in Overseas Markets

Pew's 2015 surveys show that public views on China are divided across nations and are undergoing fundamental changes. Across forty-three nations, a median of 49 per cent expressed a favourable opinion of China, while 32 per cent gave China an unfavourable rating. However, among developed nations (e.g., USA, developed EU countries), China's overall image was mostly negative; only 35 per cent of Americans had a positive view of China, while 55 per cent had a negative one. This largely negative sentiment represents a recent shift, as in 2011 half of Americans still gave China a positive rating. However, the negative attitude now seems to have taken hold; in the first quarter of 2015, roughly half or more of respondents in Italy, Germany, Poland, Spain, and France also gave China an unfavourable rating. The UK was the only EU nation whose opinion on China remained largely favourable.

In Asia, attitudes towards China differed considerably. More than two thirds held a positive opinion in the predominantly Muslim Asian nations surveyed – Pakistan, Bangladesh, Malaysia, and Indonesia – as well as a majority in Buddhist Thailand. In South Korea, a 56 per cent majority also held a favourable view, up from 46 per cent in 2013. In contrast, the percentages of negative ratings in India (39 per cent), the Philippines (58 per cent), Vietnam (78 per cent), and Japan (91 per cent) were high.

Interestingly, across all forty-three nations surveyed, the younger generation (ages 18–29 vs 50+) held a more positive perception of China, including in the USA (46 vs 26 per cent), India (34 vs 22 per cent), and the Philippines (41 vs 32 per cent). The only exception was Japan, where favourable views on China were low in both the young (11 per cent) and old (6 per cent) cohorts. As one would expect, China's negative national image tends to spill over to affect consumers' perceptions of Chinese-made products.

Studies have proposed three types of explanations driving consumers' perceptions of Chinese products, including evidence-based (e.g., product safety), individual-based (i.e., psychological) and group-based (i.e., ethnocentric) explanations. The underlying mechanisms of each type are examined here.

6.2   EVIDENCE-BASED PERCEPTION

6.2.1   *Product Safety Hazard from Chinese-Made Products*

Evidence-based perception refers to how people form images based on evidence. Aside from political evidence (e.g., war and bilateral disputes), which is beyond the scope of this book, there are two types of evidence-based perceptions that cause people to form images towards China and Chinese-made products. The first and most publicised is related to the safety hazards of Chinese-made products. As an evidence-based cause, product safety hazards elicit strong negative images of Chinese-made products. When these instances are brought into the public arena via news reports, talk shows, and blogs, the damage to the products' reputation further escalates.

Without doubt, Chinese-made products have very poor safety records, with reported hazards across product categories: from fish to milk products, from infant formula to toys, and from car tyres to building materials. Ever since China attained its 'world-factory' status, the country topped all nations in product recalls in the global economy. Eight years after the notorious Mattel lead paint toy recall, 60 per cent of toy recalls in the USA in 2014 were made-in-China products. In response, the US government set up a special agency as a monitoring institute for imports, with China being a special case that warrants attention. A similar European Watchdog agency was set up subsequently; in 2014, it issued 2,435 notifications of unsafe products, ranging from children's toys to clothing to appliances. It was reported that 64 per cent of unsafe products were made in China, matching the amount in 2013.

The Chinese government acknowledges the severity of product safety hazards and is anxious to resolve it for its export markets as well as for its own citizens. After all, product safety can lead to publicity crises that affect local stability. In recent years, China's mass media (newspapers, TV, and websites) also began investigations, reporting and exposing the country's unsafe products. Currently, food safety is among the top concerns at all levels of the government (national, provincial, municipal, and village). A root cause in product safety is corrupt activities. With the strong anti-corruption campaign in place, product safety would likely be enhanced.

It is also important to acknowledge a perceptual gap with regard to product hazards across nations. The government and consumers in China tend to perceive public health hazards (e.g., baby formula, milk, and food) to be of high priority, whereas other hazards (e.g., unhealthy material inside stuffed animals, loose parts in toys that can be swallowed, and substandard materials in clothing) are of less concern. This perceptual divide also exists in other less developed nations. To consumers in these countries, the affordability of Chinese-made products is definitely a strong selling point. Their strong price preference for Chinese products dominates concerns over what they consider to be minor safety issues. Conversely, the USA and most European governments and consumers have upheld higher standards in consumer protection across all product categories since the consumer rights movement in the 1950s. Thus, they demand stricter guidelines and institutionalised anti-hazard legislations, with penalty for violators. It is likely that this global divide on product safety will continue until the less safety sensitive consumers in China (and in other developing nations) can enjoy the same level of rights as economically developed nations.

6.2.2   *Evidence-Based Perception: Job Loss to China*

Another evidence-based perception leading to bias against China (and its products) is the 'loss of jobs' to China. For the last two decades, China has continuously attracted global manufacturing firms to relocate to the country. As a result, the supply chains that feed into China's manufacturing sectors have continued to snowball, creating enormous economies of scale in supply chain and manufacturing. Furthermore, starting in 2008, more than 1,200 global firms have set up R&D centres in China; this implies that higher-paid jobs in the manufacturing sector are also migrating out of developed economies to China. In addition, some highly paid financial jobs are also on the move. These moves have been initiated by the financial crises in the USA and the EU and further motivated by the growth potential as China modernises its financial sector.

Through a widened lens, the issue of job loss to China's growth can be seen differently. There is no doubt that Chinese imports are price competitive; with a better scale economy, China's cost advantage will continue. As a result, Chinese imports will replace higher priced products from firms in other global economies. However, even if these jobs are diversified to Asian nations with lower labour costs (e.g., Vietnam, Indonesia), job loss in developed economies (e.g., in the USA and the developed EU) will continue, as the jobs merely shift from China to the other Asian nations. As some studies have commented, global job shifts are caused by the globalisation of the supply chain in a world that is increasingly 'flat'. Thus, for global job shifts, China is a definite benefitter, but not necessarily the culprit.

When one takes a supply chain perspective to assess how a nation (e.g., the USA) can gain back the lost jobs, the answer is not straightforward. By now, globalisation has divided the manufacturing processes into a inter-locking system of specialised module-based tasks with high economic efficiency. For example, a cotton dress is the combined product of low-cost growers from Egypt, yarning and weaving mills in Pakistan, cloth-cutting shops in India, dyeing and sewing factories in China, and finishing and packaging outfits in Porta Rica before finally landing in the USA. Shifting a task module from China to the USA (or to an EU nation) means redesigning the existing supply chain. The associated costs (in both the value-chain shift and its continuous operation) can be too high to be economically viable. When a US firm intends to bear the cost and shift a task module back to the USA, it may be beaten by another US or EU competitor who chooses to continue sourcing from the existing value chain. In short, our global supply chains have evolved to a stage where any significant shift implies high transactional costs. This is one reason why Chinese Taiwan manufacturers failed to shift their production bases from

China to other Asian economies when its former leader Chen Suibian urged them to do so a decade ago.

Interestingly, there is a distinction among the generation cohorts on the issue of job loss. A Pews survey showed that the younger generation holds a broader global view (Wike, Stokes, and Poushter, 2015). While they do suffer from job losses, they tend to attribute the root cause of such losses to their government's lack of global vision in building their nation's competitiveness compared with China. Their more positive attitude towards China may also come from a buyer lens; they are heavy users of personal electronic products, in which China is globally strong, offering highly affordable products. In comparison, the older generational cohort tends to hold a more negative image towards Chinese-made products. We shall return to this generational divide later in the chapter.

6.3   INDIVIDUAL- AND GROUP-BASED PERCEPTIONS ON CHINA AND CHINESE-MADE PRODUCTS

6.3.1   Individual Perception

The global proliferation of products made in China implies that most people around the world have used at least some Chinese-made products. Personal experiences are powerful inputs for individuals when forming their attitudes, and when these experiences are repeated over time, they form an enduring attitude towards Chinese-made products. These attitudes will be further shaped by media reports and experiences from their friends.

Over time, these attitudes function as anchors (also labelled as stereotypes) that are difficult to change and may not co-evolve with the reality. Psychology studies show that, once formed, these anchors are defended from changes by one's personality traits or one's perceived social roles (Fiske, 2000). In daily life, these stereotypes are used as sense-making tools (Macrae and Bodenhausen, 2000) and time and energy savers (Sherman, Macrae, and Bodenhausen, 2000) so information can be easily identified, recalled, and used. They operate as decision-making shortcuts, reducing one's daily cognitive demand.

Studies have confirmed that the made-in-China image operates similarly, affecting a person's daily purchase decisions. As a stereotype (Gürhan-Canli and Maheswaran, 2000; Tse and Gorn, 1993), the made-in-China image enables individuals to give meaning to the products they see (Taylor, 1981) and thus evaluate and decide whether to buy these products (Gürhan-Canli and Maheswaran, 2000).

Based on the previous discussion, consumers could be expected to associate made-in-China products with product quality and safety concerns (Tan and Tse, 2010) and accordingly to engage in more careful evaluations of such products (Verlegh and Steenkamp, 1999), balancing their advantages (often lower price) against their potential disadvantages (inferior quality, potential risks) when making a purchase decision. As a result, consumers from developed economies would likely make unfavourable evaluations of Chinese-made products.

6.3.2 Group-Based Perception: Ethnocentrism

Consumers do not act alone. The perceptions of others, especially their friends and relatives, play a significant role when they evaluate products (Klein, 2002). In the case of Chinese-made products, two social norms are salient. First, as discussed earlier, there is a shared view among consumers in developed economies that Chinese-made products are inferior. In addition, another powerful social norm, consumer ethnocentrism, may affect consumer purchase decisions.

Shimp and Sharma (1987) conceptualise ethnocentrism as 'beliefs held by American (or any other country) consumers about the appropriateness, indeed morality, of purchasing foreign-made products' (p. 280). This is a motivational bias, in that an ethnocentric consumer may prefer domestic over foreign-made products despite contradicting knowledge on these products' price and quality (Klein, 2002). Since its conceptualisation, studies have validated the salience of this effect in different countries, products, and consumption contexts (Balabanis and Diamantopoulos, 2004; Pappu, Quester, and Cooksey, 2007).

Studies have investigated how ethnocentrism operates and its antecedents (e.g., patriotism, national animosity) across product categories and countries (Ouellet, 2007; Sharma, 2010). Consumer ethnocentrism is confirmed to be a deep-rooted motivation, carrying social meaning and causing a person to resist changes (Schneider, 2004). Studies have shown that changing group-based stereotypes require major shifts in key cultural norms, such as common interests and humanity appeals (Wyer, 1998). Thus, changing consumers' ethnocentrism is difficult and uncommon.

Ethnocentrism emerges when the focal foreign country (in this case, China) is perceived to be a threat against one's own country (Balabanis and Diamantopoulos, 2004; Leong et al., 2008). When this happens, consumers will ignore the objective attributes of the products, rendering consumer ethnocentrism salient (Sharma, Shimp, and Shin, 1995). This effect is especially strong in credence products (products that cannot be objectively experienced) and frequently-purchased products (e.g., fast-moving consumer goods) (Ouellet, 2007). Studies also show that, while product experiences may reduce the effect of ethnocentrism, they do not nullify it.

Tensions between countries are rampant around the world, resulting from territorial disputes, economic competition, and diplomatic disagreements (Riefler and Diamantopoulos, 2007). These 'remnants of antipathy related to previous or ongoing military, political or economic events' (Klein, Ettenson, and Morris, 1998, p. 90) represent a consumer's animosity against the focal country that in turn accentuates one's ethnocentric tendencies. China's expanding global footprint has sparked a range of concerns and potential threats among neighbouring countries (Pew Research, 2014). Its emerging perception as the world's second largest economy (Wike, Stokes, and Poushter,

2015) with increasing global involvement reinforces consumers' feelings towards China as a potential economic threat.

Thus, some consumers from developed economies will likely assume an ethnocentric bias when they consider buying Chinese-made products. They may justify their biases by associating China's economic rise with high unemployment in their home countries. Thus, they attribute acts of economic animosity (Leong et al., 2008) against their own country to China. Motivated to 'make a difference', they prefer domestic over Chinese-made products to support their own country. In the USA, this form of collective sentiment has appeared in the public media (e.g., Bremmer, 2010). Therefore, the more ethnocentric views a person holds, the more unfavourable his or her preference would be towards Chinese-made products.

The previous discussion points to three types of immense attitudinal challenges (evidenced-, individual-, and group-based perceptions) Chinese-made products face in developed economies. However, the world is evolving continuously, resulting in shifts in each of the three perceptual domains, as discussed later.

6.4 PERCEPTUAL CHANGES

6.4.1 Changes in Evidence-Based Perceptions

With regard to evidence-based perceptions, Chinese-made products have gradually improved their safety records because of several key factors. First, different levels of Chinese government (national, provincial, municipal, and village) regard product safety as their top concern. This concern is so strong that there is a rumour that China's state council in Beijing has to manage its own farms (vegetable, fish, pigs, etc.) and logistic supply to ensure that the food the top officials eat is safe (Fang, 2015). This drives them to assume a strong hand against any unsafe products. Further, the recent anti-corruption movement (started in 2017) in the government helps break corruptive rings of officials and suppliers on product safety. The *willingness to act* by top officials is crucial to control food safety in a complex social-institutional context like China.

In addition, the media also offers a good deal of help. Through mass and social media, both on- and off-line, and with no obvious policy against their reporting (except for fabricated stories), product safety hazards are duly reported and viralled across China. This further raises the public's concern and puts pressure on the government to act upon these instances. We hasten to point out that the current focus on improving product safety is on food safety, so safety issues in other products remain severe.

The quality of Chinese products is improving for yet another reason. The weak global economy tends to drive away weak brands and those with inferior quality. In China, middle-income families (Wang, 2010) are on the rise, so lower-quality products with super-low prices are gradually being replaced. These changes are not obvious to consumers in developed economies, but the gradual decline in inferior products is obvious in China.

Interestingly, the rise of some Chinese brands may play a salient role in improving the image of Chinese products. The strong performance of Lenovo (the firm that bought IBM in 2004) demonstrates that some Chinese brands and products are of good quality. More recently, the rise of Huawei among the top mobile phones has helped to change perceptions of Chinese products. To some consumers, selected Chinese-made products, such as personal electronics, are highly acceptable. Thus, the continuous globalisation of Chinese firms is indeed a double-edged sword. Being on the global stage, Chinese-made products are faced with strong and harsh scrutiny, so that both faults and successes will be magnified. If the Chinese-made products are successfully launched globally with good quality, they will serve as a major image enhancer. In particular, some people believe that China's high-speed rail can be a potential game changer in Chinese products perception on a global scale.

6.4.2   Changes in Individual-Based Perception

We postulate that individual-based perceptions are also currently changing. In addition to the quality improvement of some rising Chinese brands, global travel and the Internet have shrunk the physical and perceptual distance among nations, thus expanding people's worldview and eliciting their interest to interact with people from other cultures. Flynn (2005, p. 817) labels this effect as cultural openness, or 'the willingness to interact with cultures other than one's own'. For China, its cultural distinctiveness and diversity (regional and multiracial diversity), its geographic and scenic attractions, and its historical legacy and relics (Great Wall, Forbidden City, etc.) are well-received by many around the world.

Consumers who are culturally open are receptive towards other cultures, including those cultures' people, values, and practices (Appelbaum and Robinson, 2005; Axford, 2005). Flynn (2005) showed that cultural openness is salient in adjusting a person's stereotypes. A person who is more receptive will have the capacity to absorb new information and change existing biases. Such a person will also develop altruistic empathy towards other countries. Accordingly, differences and diversity may become points of interest rather than points of conflict for these individuals.

While stereotypes typically discourage exposure to new and conflicting information, the openness explanation posits that putting an individual in contact with the object in dispute encourages a person to process conflicting information, subsequently leading to a change in stereotypes (Pettigrew and Tropp, 2006). As a result, a culturally open consumer will likely be more receptive, and thus more tolerant and accepting, towards Chinese-made products.

In a three-nation (the USA, UK, and Australia) study with 400 consumers in each country, Hung (2015) examined the effect of cultural openness on purchase intention towards Chinese-made products. They found that culturally open consumers are significantly more positive in their purchase intent towards Chinese-made

products. This effect is universal across the three developed economies in the study. In sum, there is increasing evidence to suggest that,
although 'made in China' is a salient negative stereotype affecting
individual consumers, increasing cultural openness is revising it, as
cultural openness increasingly becomes an attribute of a pluralistic
society (Guiso et al. 2006).

6.4.3   Changes in Group-Based Perception

What about the effect of consumer ethnocentrism? How can this
group-based bias be mitigated? A number of approaches are known
to reduce a person's group-based stereotypes. Specifically, these
include removing the fears that underlie the stereotype. Consumer
ethnocentrism emerges when consumers feel the need to make
a difference for their home country in the face of supposed economic
threats from China.

Reducing ethnocentrism can be achieved by promoting world-
mindedness, or 'a world-view on the problems of humanity' (Sampson
and Smith, 1957; Skinner, 1988). World-mindedness is a state of mind
in which consumers use humankind as the primary reference group
instead of their respective nationalities (Rawwas, Rajendran, and
Wuehrer, 1996). In so doing, a person will take a broadened perspective
so that the developmental needs of China and the need of its workers
will be considered against potential job losses in one's own country. In
the end, the consumer may arrive at a more balanced view of the
world, and, accordingly, the potential economic threats posed by
Chinese firms and their products will not be as alarming to the person.

In the literature, world-minded consumers have interests in and
knowledge of international affairs, the salient attributes for consensus
development (Gomberg, 1994) in our pluralising world. The proliferation of the new media has given rise to an informed and interconnected world (Appelbaum and Robinson, 2005). Through these media,
a consumer's perspective on the world (worldview) is continuously
broadened, allowing the person to learn about and participate in global
issues and events.

With this broadened view, the developing countries formerly seen as 'poor nations that are irrelevant to us' may be re-evaluated as 'nations whose needs and growth are part of our future'. This perceptual shift will dampen pre-existing stereotypes. Instead of assuming the 'in-group' versus 'out-group' approach, world-mindedness stimulates consumers to use a 'we' perspective. Then, threat perceptions and ethnocentric biases against Chinese-made products will be reduced. Through world-mindedness, the negative effects of consumer ethnocentrism on purchase intentions for Chinese-made products can be alleviated.

In the same three-nation (the USA, UK, and Australia) study mentioned earlier, Hung (2015) found that world-minded consumers are significantly more positive in their purchase intent towards Chinese-made products than those who are less world-minded. This effect is universal across the three developed economies in the study. Global polls (www.Gallup.com) reports that people's world-mindedness has continuously expanded to include the issues and needs of developing economies. Similar results from Pew Survey (Pew Research, 2014) reveal that the feeling of 'one-world-ness' is growing and is increasingly shared by people of different nations. Whether this trend is driven by the need for environmental conservation or international peace, a gradually broadening perspective is emerging (Appelbaum and Robinson, 2005). In sum, the trend of global-mindedness brings relief to collective biases against Chinese-made products.

As revealed in the 2014 Pew study, the younger generation cohorts of consumers in all nations (except Japan) are much more positive towards China than those of the respective older generation. This phenomenon shows the effect of growing global-mindedness among the younger generation. If this trend continues, Chinese-made products should receive more objective evaluations in the future.

6.4.4 New Chinese Brands and Their Effects on China's Image

In addition to the previously mentioned image improvements regarding Chinese-made products, two brand successes further enhance the perceptions of Chinese products on a global scale. These include Xiaomi in the mobile phone market and Alibaba in global e-commerce. These two brands succeed in highly competitive markets and against strong global players. Their successes help position China-made products and Chinese firms in a new light.

Xiaomi has leapfrogged to attain global respect in its low-end mobile phones among intense global competition. Its founder and chairman, Mr Lei Jun, defines the firm as an Internet rather than a hardware firm, yet Xiaomi's product portfolio (smartphones, tablets, laptops, smart TVs, and home devices) has received high regard and brought in USD18 billion sales in 2017. By 2018, it is the world's fourth largest smartphone firm (see Figure 6.1). Xiaomi has 15,000 employees in China, India, Malaysia, and Singapore and is expanding to other countries such as Indonesia, the Philippines, and South Africa. Its major markets include China (62.3 per cent), India (19.6 per cent), Indonesia (7.1 per cent), Russia (2.7 per cent), and the Ukraine (0.7 per cent) as of 2017 (Heingartner, 2017).

Among the income groups served by different brands of smartphones, 40 per cent of Apple users are high-income consumers,

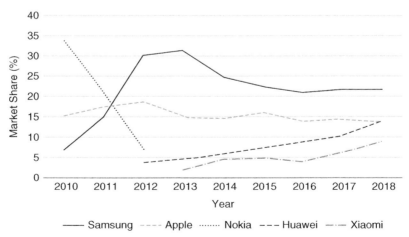

FIGURE 6.1 Smartphone market share worldwide, 2010–18
Source: Statcounter (2018)

compared to Samsung with 31 per cent, Huawei with 20 per cent, and Xiaomi with only about 12 per cent. High-income customers tend to own high-end devices and spend more resources (time, money) on apps and accessories, so these consumers are valuable to Xiaomi. To capture this profitable segment, Xiaomi has strategically increased its focus on high-end devices and set up convenient mobile phone accessory stores throughout Europe. Should these accessory stores be accepted, Xiaomi's image (and later its phone) will likely escalate. It is foreseeable that Xiaomi may gradually gain higher-income consumers and become a strong global brand.

As another example, Alibaba is truly a path-breaker in global e-commerce. Its founder, Jack Ma, has become a well-known global business leader. His wit and business wisdom can easily match those of any Chinese business leader in history. Anyone who traces his background would be attracted by his unorthodox way of leading Alibaba, his provocative yet insightful vision for the future of the business, and his unparalleled success in spearheading Alibaba to become one of the most successful e-commerce firms worldwide.

Under his leadership, Alibaba has broken record after record. On 19 September 2014, the firm's initial public offering was at USD25 billion – the highest in world history – and Alibaba's market value reached USD231 billion. As of June 2018, Alibaba's market capitalisation stood at USD542 billion, making the firm one of the top ten most valuable and biggest companies in the world. By January 2018, Alibaba became the second Asian company to break the USD500 billion valuation mark, after Tencent. These outstanding successes reflect Jack Ma's innovative mindset, which involves relentlessly charging forward with multiple successful business units including Taobao, TMall, Alibaba Cloud, Ali Express, Alipay (e-payment platform), AliMusic, Alibaba Pictures, AliHealth, AliSports, and so on.

By now, Xiaomi and Alibaba have become legends in their respective industries. Their challenges and successes go beyond the scope of this book, yet we hasten to point out that these two exemplary firms have helped improve people's perception of Chinese products and Chinese firms. Strong evidence of these changing views can be found in their joint venture partners. Xiaomi has joint ventures with Philips Lighting (2016), Nokia (2017), and global phone service provider Three (2018). Alibaba has joint ventures with global leaders such as Starbucks (the biggest coffee roaster in Shanghai, 2018) and Marriott International (2018). It also has joint ventures with Mail.ru (Russian gaming firm, 2018) and Magafon (Russian e-distributor, 2018).

6.5   CONCLUSION

This chapter highlights how consumers from different economies perceive and evaluate Chinese-made products through a perceptual lens. It delineates findings from studies and industry reports and points out the challenges that Chinese firms face as they globally market their products. The genuine weakness in Chinese products is duly recognised. Following more than a decade of poor safety records and inferior quality, Chinese-made unsafe products are of global concern. Over time, these instances have created a justifiably unfavourable perception of Chinese-made products on a global scale. There are, however, some evidence of positive changes. First, the problems related to food safety are heavily scrutinised, both within and outside China. Consumers in China deserve a safer consumption environment, and thus it is comforting to know that the Chinese government is actively dealing with the issues and their underlying causes. Second, there are two salient social trends that help consumers revise their perceptions towards Chinese-made products: cultural openness and world-mindedness. As the trends of increasing interests in other cultures and seeing the world in a broadened view continue, unjustified biases against Chinese-made products may be reduced in the future.

Third, we argue that there will be a continual divide among consumers in developed and emerging economies with regard to consumer rights. Sensitivity to and standards of product safety are closely tied to differences in consumer rights across these two groups of economies. In the USA and developed EU countries, materials inside stuffed toys and lead paint are important concerns, while Chinese (or Indian or Brazilian) consumers may not see them as serious. Until such differences are reduced, it is likely that designers and manufacturers in China will not be as sensitive to such concerns as desired by consumers in other countries. In sum, while we believe that tighter policy executions will 'clean up' safety hazards in China and help remove toxic materials from food and other products, product safety issues will continue to dampen the acceptance of Chinese-made products.

Other factors that are salient to the images of Chinese-made products include rising labour costs (raising questions about whether China will remain the world factory), worker welfare (how Chinese workers are treated), and environmental sustainability (whether green manufacturing processes are used). These will be discussed further in other chapters, especially in Chapter 7.

REFERENCES

Appelbaum, R. P. and Robinson, W. I. (2005). *Critical Globalization Studies.* New York: Routledge.

Axford, B. (2005). 'Critical Globalization Studies and a Network Perspective on Global Civil Society'. In *Critical Globalization Studies*, R. P. Appelbaum and W. I Robinson, eds. New York: Routledge, 187–96.

Balabanis, G. and Diamantopoulos, A. (2004). Domestic country bias, country-of-origin effects, and consumer ethnocentrism: a multidimensional unfolding approach. *Journal of the Academy of Marketing Science*, 32(1): 80–95.

Bremmer, I. (2010). China V.S. America: fight of the century. *Prospect.* 22 March. Retrieved 3 October 2012. www.prospectmagazine.co.uk/magazine/china-vs-america-fight-of-the-century.

Fang, S. (2015). The party has its own, safe food supply in China. *Epoch Times.* 1 October. Retrieved 12 July 2019. www.theepochtimes.com/the-party-has-its-own-safe-food-supply-in-china_1498024.html.

Fiske, S. T. (2000). Stereotyping, prejudice, and discrimination at the seam between the centuries: evolution, culture, mind, and brain. *European Journal of Social Psychology*, 30: 299–322.

Flynn, F. J. (2005). Having an open mind: the impact of openness to experience on interracial attitudes and impression formation. *Journal of Personality and Social Psychology*, 88(5): 816–26.

Gomberg, P. (1994). Universalism and optimism. *Ethics*, 104(3): 536–57.

Guiso, L., Sapienza, P., and Zingales, L. (2006). Does culture affect economic outcomes? *Journal of Economic Perspectives*, 20(2): 23–48.

Gürhan-Canli, Z. and Maheswaran, D. (2000). Determinants of country-of-origin evaluations. *Journal of Consumer Research*, 27(June): 96–108.

Heingartner, D. (2017). Xiaomi on the ascent, eyes new markets with high-end Android phones. *Newzoo*. 5 October. Retrieved 12 July 2019. https://newzoo.com/insights/articles/xiaomi-ascent-eyes-new-markets-high-end-android-phones.

Hung, K. (2015). 'Repairing the Made-in-China Image in the US and UK: Effects of Government-Supported Advertising'. In *International Public Relations and Public Diplomacy: Communication and Engagement*, G. Golan, S-U. Yang, and D. Kinsey, eds. New York: Peter Lang Publishing, 209–28.

Klein, J. G. (2002). Us versus them, or us versus everyone? Delineating consumer aversion to foreign goods. *Journal of International Business Studies*, 33(2): 345–63.

Klein, J. G., Ettenson, R., and Morris, M. D. (1998). The animosity model of foreign product purchase: an empirical test in the People's Republic of China. *Journal of Marketing*, 62(1): 89–100.

Leong, S. M., Cote, J. A., Ang, S. H., et al. (2008). Understanding consumer animosity in an international crisis: nature, antecedents, and consequences. *Journal of International Business Studies*, 39(6): 996–1009.

Macrae, C. N. and Bodenhausen, G. V. (2000). Social cognition: thinking categorically about others. *Annual Review of Psychology*, 51: 93–120.

Ouellet, J.-F. (2007). Consumer racism and its effects on domestic cross-ethnic product purchase: an empirical test in the United States, Canada, and France. *Journal of Marketing*, 71(1): 113–28.

Pappu, R., Quester, P. G., and Cooksey, R. W. (2007). Country image and consumer-based brand equity: relationships and implications for international marketing. *Journal of International Business Studies*, 38(5): 726–45.

Pettigrew, T. F. and Tropp, L. R. (2006). A meta-analytic test of intergroup contact theory. *Journal of Personality and Social Psychology*, 90(5): 751–83.

Pew Research. (2014). Pervasive gloom about the world economy. *Pew Research Center*. 12 July. Retrieved 21 September 2012. http://pewresearch.org/pubs/2306/global-attitudes-economic-glum-crisis-capitalism-european-union-united-states-china-brazil-outlook-work-ethic-recession-satisfaction-gloomy.

Rawwas, M. Y. A., Rajendran, K. N., and Wuehrer, G. A. (1996). The influence of worldmindedness and nationalism on consumer evaluation of domestic and foreign products. *International Marketing Review*, 13(2): 20–38.

Riefler, P. and Diamantopoulos, A. (2007). Consumer animosity: a literature review and a reconsideration of its measurement. *International Marketing Review*, 24 (1), 87–119.

Sampson, D. L. and Smith, H. P. (1957). A scale to measure world-minded attitudes. *The Journal of Social Psychology*, 45(1): 99–106.

Schneider, D. J. (2004). *The Psychology of Stereotyping*. New York: The Guilford Press.

Sharma, P. (2010). Country of origin effects in developed and emerging markets: exploring the contrasting roles of materialism and value consciousness. *Journal of International Business Studies*, 42(2): 285–306.

Sharma, S., Shimp, T. A., and Shin, J. (1995). Consumer ethnocentrism: a test of antecedents and moderators. *Journal of the Academy of Marketing Science*, 23 (1): 26–37.

Sherman, J. W., Macrae, C. N., and Bodenhausen, G. V. (2000). Attention and stereotyping: cognitive constraints on the construction of meaningful social impressions. *European Review of Social Psychology*, 11(1): 145–75.

Shimp, T. A. and Sharma, S. (1987). Consumer ethnocentrism: construction and validation of the CETSCALE. *Journal of Marketing Research*, 24(August): 280–9.

Skinner, K. A. (1988). Internationalism and the early years of the Japanese Peace Corps. *International Journal of Intercultural Relations*, 12: 317–26.

Statcounter. (2018). Mobile vendor market share worldwide, electronic dataset. *Statecounter*. Retrieved 12 July 2019. http://gs.statcounter.com/vendor-market-share/mobile.

Tan, P. and Tse, D. K. (2010). Becoming truly global: Which Chinese brands can succeed in affluent global markets and how. *Harvard Business Review* (8): 13–17.

Taylor, S. E. (1981). 'A Categorization Approach to Stereotyping'. In *Cognitive Process in Stereotyping and Intergroup Behaviour*, D. L. Hamilton, ed. Hillsdale, NJ: Erlbaum, 83–114.

Tse, D. K. and Gorn, G. J. (1993). An experiment on the salience of country-of-origin in the era of global brands. *Journal of International Marketing*, 1(1): 57–76.

Verlegh, P. W. J. and Steenkamp, J.-B. E. M. (1999). A review and meta-analysis of country-of-origin research. *Journal of Economic Psychology*, 20: 521–46.

Wang, H. H. (2010). *The Chinese Dream: The Rise of the World's Largest Middle Class and What It Means to You*. Brande: Bestseller Press.

Wike, Y. R., Stokes, B., and Poushter, J. (2015). Global publics back U.S. on fighting ISIS, but are critical of post-9/11 torture: Asian nations mostly support TPP, defense pivot – but also value economic ties with China. *Pew Research Center*. 23 June. Retrieved 12 July 2019. www.pewresearch.org/global/2015/06/23/glo bal-publics-back-u-s-on-fighting-isis-but-are-critical-of-post-911-torture/.

Wyer, R. S., Jr. (1998). *Stereotype Activation and Inhibition*. Mahwah, NJ: L. Erlbaum Associates.

7   Corporate Social Responsibility

7.1   INTRODUCTION

Many news reports over the past decade have highlighted the poor corporate practices at Chinese firms that have led to worker suicides (e.g., Foxconn), production of harmful products (e.g., Changsheng Biotechnology), and environmental pollution (e.g., Zijin Mining). These events have caused major concerns in both domestic and overseas markets. In addition, they represent barriers to Chinese firms attempting to globalise in developed or emerging economies. This chapter addresses the issue of CSR among globalising Chinese firms. In spite of Chinese firms' poor history and bad publicity in this area, a recent study shows that globalising Chinese firms, especially the SOEs in overseas markets, are now engaged in CSR best practices as a result of government initiatives (Sarkis, Ni, and Zhu, 2011). In contrast, however, local SMEs in China still lag behind in their CSR efforts.

This chapter examines the development of CSR in Chinese firms, including their drivers and their current state. To prevent Chinese firms from having profit maximisation as their sole objective, the Chinese government has positioned CSR activities as an area central to the country's stability and future growth. It has developed guidelines and encouraged firms to adopt them in corporate policies and activities. The chapter ends by examining the CSR practices adopted by Huawei, a major Chinese firm, in its overseas operations.

7.1.1   CSR in Contemporary Global Context

CSR signals an important development in management thinking. Whereas its salience can be traced back to the early twentieth century, its widespread implementation is more recent, as firms around the world have gradually moved towards integrating it into their strategies and operations. A major driver for firms to seriously adopt CSR is the stakeholder theory (Donaldson and Preston, 1995; Freeman, 1984; Mitchell, Agle, and Wood, 1997). This theory suggests that, in addition to meeting shareholders' desire to maximise a firm's financial returns, a firm needs to be ethically responsible to all stakeholders (including employees, customers, suppliers, interest groups, and government bodies) that may be affected by the firm's corporate values and activities.

Scholars posit that, while CSR activities incur additional costs, successful businesses can create a win–win situation by balancing their impacts on society as they satisfy the financial interests of shareholders (Bansal, 2005). Such a win–win situation was illustrated by a fifteen-country public survey carried out by the Reputation Institute, a global consulting firm based in New York. Almost half of the survey respondents indicated that their perceptions of an MNC were based on its CSR practices. These perceptions, in turn, drive the public's willingness to buy from, recommend, work for, or invest in an MNC (Smith, 2012). Thus, the survey findings show that CSR can effectively improve the relational gap between an MNC and the general public. In other words, giving back to local communities through CSR may enhance the general public's trust and goodwill towards the MNC. As such, CSR not only is good for society, but also is a salient contributor to corporate success and sustainability.

Currently, CSR takes into account the social, economic, and environmental impacts of a firm's operations. This broader conceptualisation of a firm's roles as outlined in the UN Global Compact in 2000 ensures that corporate activities support sustainable development for future generations. Today, many publicly listed firms include their CSR efforts in their annual reports.

7.1.2   UN Global Compact

The UN Global Compact is a UN initiative to encourage firms around the world to adopt and implement socially responsible policies and behaviours. In particular, this initiative focuses on ten principles involving business activities that are deemed necessary to support broader UN goals, such as the Millennium Development Goals (2000–2015) and the Sustainable Development Goals (2016–2030). The UN Global Compact has 13,000 corporate participants and other stakeholders from more than 170 countries that are supportive and invested in this initiative. Interested readers may refer to the following UN website for details: www.unglobalcompact.org/.

The UN Global Compact originally addressed business activities related to three areas: human rights, labour standards, and the environment that firms around the world should uphold. During the first Global Compact Leaders' Summit in 2004, Kofi Annan, then-UN Secretary-General, announced the addition of a fourth area, anti-corruption, to support the UN Convention against Corruption. The following list outlines the ten principles under the four core areas of the UN Global Compact.

Human Rights
- Principle 1: Businesses should support and respect the protection of internationally proclaimed human rights; and
- Principle 2: make sure that they are not complicit in human rights abuses.

Labour
- Principle 3: Businesses should uphold freedom of association and effective recognition of the right to collective bargaining;
- Principle 4: the elimination of all forms of forced and compulsory labour;
- Principle 5: the effective abolition of child labour; and
- Principle 6: the elimination of discrimination in respect of employment and occupation.

Environment
- Principle 7: Businesses should support a precautionary approach to environmental challenges;
- Principle 8: undertake initiatives to promote greater environmental responsibility; and
- Principle 9: encourage the development and diffusion of environmentally friendly technologies.

Anti-Corruption
- Principle 10: Businesses should work against all forms of corruption, including extortion and bribery.

The UN Global Compact is not a regulatory instrument. Instead, it is a forum for discussion among governments, corporations, labour groups, civil society organisations, and other stakeholders to maintain a sustainable world. Given the diversity in business systems, cultures, and societies internationally, the ten principles and their objectives and activities are flexible, allowing them to be adapted to fit a firm's structure and governance. In other words, CSR is a contextualised paradigm that embodies cultural sensitivities and social institutional properties, which need to be understood within the country in which a firm operates.

7.1.2   Development of CSR in China

Whereas CSR is a Western concept, the 'responsible business' concept has a 2,500-year tradition in China. Strongly influenced by Confucian values, Chinese merchants adopted the 'Confucian Trader' ideal that honoured morality, sincerity, and benevolence. They pursued a responsible and harmonious approach in their business relations (Wang and Juslin, 2009).

This tradition lost its prominence as a principle for trading over the generations, especially during times of war. Nevertheless, China's SOEs, with their socialistic orientation, operated as small communities that provided housing, school, and medication to their members (Wang and Juslin, 2009). This socialistic notion lost its influence after 1984, when private and joint-venture enterprises began to flourish and compete with the SOEs in China. Under the economic liberalisation policy, the main objective of all firms was to maximise profitability. Thus, SOEs cut back many of their social responsibility programmes in order to remain economically viable.

The Western concept of CSR was introduced to China during the mid-1990s amid concerns over the labour conditions in China and other emerging economies (e.g., child labour) when many MNCs out-source their manufacturing operations to China. MNCs such as Carrefour, Nike, and GE demanded their Chinese suppliers meet more stringent auditing standards that included not only production quality, product safety, and risk management, but also CSR efforts such as environmental protection and good labour practices (Wang and Juslin, 2009). The suppliers that performed well on the audit were supported, while those that performed poorly lost their contracts. Chinese firms accepted these demands reluctantly. The new demands were seen by Chinese businesspeople either as requirements imposed by foreign firms who did not understand the reality of Chinese society or as hurdles brought on by China's ascension to the WTO (Hung, Tse, and Cheng, 2012).

Over time, Chinese firms accepted CSR practices, especially with the encouragement of the government. Successful Chinese suppliers improved their processes to meet these auditing requirements, and, at the same time, they also accepted the need for international labour laws and ethical practices. Some also integrated socially responsible behaviour into their operations, which helped to address the employment shortage in the country. Meanwhile, other stakeholders such as consumers in China also become sensitised to firms' social responsibilities (see Figure 7.1).

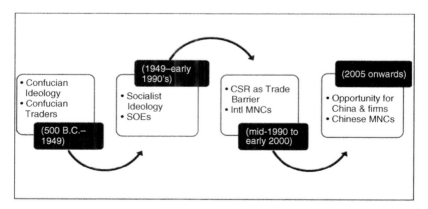

FIGURE 7.1 Timeline for the development of CSR in China

7.2   CSR WITH CHINESE CHARACTERISTICS

7.2.1   *CSR Dimensions*

A recent survey of firms identified two indigenous dimensions of Chinese CSR: employment (e.g., increase job opportunities, ease national employment pressure) and social stability and progress (e.g., ensure social stability and harmony, promote patriotism and national prosperity) (Xu and Yang, 2010). In addition to environmental safeguards, customer protection, and employee welfare, these expanded dimensions are firm efforts that support the nation's political and societal stability and are referred to as 'socialism with Chinese characteristics', 'Beijing Consensus', and the 'Chinese Model of Development' (Tang and Li, 2011). Indeed, the country's emphases on employment and social stability is at the core of China's national development plan. These indigenous dimensions, and especially employment, are strongly supported by the Chinese people (Xu and Yang, 2010). A survey of CSR professionals showed that the employment dimension was highly salient, with 62 per cent of respondents indicating that it is one of the three most important CSR emphases in China (CSR Asia and Embassy of Sweden, 2014).

7.2.2   *The Government as a Key CSR Driver*

Rather than operating alone, businesses form a network of relationships with various stakeholders within a community. In most Western countries, consumers, activists, non-governmental organisations (NGOs), and the media pressure firms to carry out CSR activities. In China, however, it is the government that forms the major force driving the country's CSR efforts in firms. This is not surprising, as the government is known to be the most significant influencer of China's industrial practices. Firms thus regard their CSR activities not as a strategic choice, but as a requirement from the government. As of recent years, CSR is fast becoming a social demand that embodies China's national and public interests (Matten and Moon, 2008).

Among government initiatives that have been put forth, the most important one is the Harmonious Society Policy proposed by the National People's Congress in 2005. This policy revises China's unidimensional emphasis on economic growth from 1980 to 2005 to also embrace societal balance and harmony. This is seen as a 'natural' progression to adjust China's growing wealth disparity among its country's regions as well as among citizen groups over the past thirty years. According to UN statistics, the poorest 20 per cent of China's citizens account for only 4.7 per cent of China's total income, while the richest 20 per cent account for more than half (Cody, 2005). The gaps between rich and poor, between urban and rural, and between coastal and inland regions can feed social unrest, riots, and violent protests (Cody, 2005).

In addition, China needs corporate CSR to mitigate the serious environmental damages inflicted by firms over the past decades due to the single-minded quest for corporate profitability. The World Bank estimated that the damage caused by water and air pollution in China amounted to between 3.5 and 8 per cent of China's GDP (World Bank, 2007). The environmental degradation is highlighted in the infamous documentary *Under the Dome*, which drew millions of people into the debate (Hatton, 2015).

Addressing the core issues of social disparity and environmental damages required long-term education backed by a series of public-policy initiatives. First, the Chinese government took a top-down interventionist approach to ensure corporate CSR aligns with the country's public interests. As a result, CSR was instituted into the Chinese Company Law (2006) and the Labour Contract Law (2008), making CSR practices a 'must' for all firms. Next, the state-owned Assets Supervision and Administration Commission of the State Council issued an important directive on 'Guidelines to the State-owned Enterprises Directly Managed under the Central Government on Fulfilling Corporate Social Responsibilities' in 2008. Furthermore, China's twelfth (2011–15) and thirteenth (2016–20) five-year plans emphasised the development of green energy; reduced carbon emission; and equity in healthcare, education, and employment. These efforts are part of China's push for a more harmonious society.

SOEs are leading firms in corporate CSR. State Grid, an energy supplier ranked among the Fortune Global 500 top ten, issued the first SOE CSR report the same year the corporate law came into effect in 2006. The Shanghai and Shenzhen stock exchanges also provided guidelines for publicly listed companies on CSR (Schmidpeter and Stehr, 2015). By 2013, 75 per cent of SOEs included CSR in their strategic objectives.

For private firms in China, CSR is regarded as a form of relationship-building with different levels of government. Aside from activities that encourage employment and social stability, there are overwhelming supports for disaster relief, and there are good reasons for these. First, these efforts are highly profiled in mass media and thus provide good publicity (Wang and Chaudhri, 2009). Second, they reflect well on the owners' ethical values. Some private firms also support philanthropy projects in education and care for the elderly (Tang and Li, 2011), as well as short-term projects initiated by local and regional governments, such as tree-planting. They contribute to firm's relationships with various levels of government.

Collectively, these governmental efforts help firms improve their CSR activities in China. A study by the Chinese Academy of Social Sciences showed that the top firms in China, including the top 100 SOEs, top 100 private firms, and top 100 foreign firms improved their CSR practices substantially over a seven-year period, from a score of 15.2 in 2009 to a score of 34.4 in 2015 (Fang, 2015). However, around 50 per cent of the firms surveyed remained observers of CSR or declined to provide such information. Many of these firms are SMEs. As in other countries, considerable work remains to be done to bring about a society-wide endorsement of CSR.

7.3   CSR POLICY IN CHINA

7.3.1   *Chinese CSR Policy and Global Standard*

From a strategic perspective, there is a need for third-party endorsement to align China's CSR efforts with international standards. This is recognised by China's State Council in an official document titled 'Guidance on Social Responsibility', which came into effect in January 2016. The document aimed at assisting Chinese firms to integrate CSR activities into their policies and planning. It outlines six core subjects identical to those outlined in ISO 26000:2010, the international standard for CSR that the Chinese government participated in its negotiation and writing. The six core subjects are: human rights, labour practices, environment preservation, fair operating practices, consumer rights, and community involvement and development.

Similar to the UN Global Compact, the 'Guidance on Social Responsibility' also has three core subjects concerning human rights, labour standards, and environment concerns, respectively, although the specific issues under the core subjects differ between the two guidelines. For example, human rights constitute a highly sensitive issue to Chinese and foreign MNCs operating in China. While the rights to survival and development are considered the most essential human rights in China, in the West they typically include one's rights to freedom, safety, and equality (Tang and Li, 2011). Nevertheless, as a member of the UN Human Rights Council, China has a responsibility to adopt a framework that ensures that corporations respect human rights in accordance with the UN principles.

The core subject of fair operating practices outlined in China's 'Guidance on Social Responsibility' is similar to the UN Global Compact's subject of anti-corruption, but its scope is broader. With regard to consumer issues and community involvement and development, there are some differences between the two guidelines. Consumers constitute a special group of stakeholders, and consumer rights are often treated as an issue independent of CSR issues in many developed countries. The core subject of community involvement and development will be discussed in the next section. The following outlines the core subjects and issues formalised by China's 'Guidance on Social Responsibility'.

Core Subject: Human Rights
- Issue 1: Civil and political rights
- Issue 2: Economic, social, and cultural rights
- Issue 3: Fundamental principles and rights at work

Core Subject: Labour Practices
- Issue 1: Employment and employment relationships
- Issue 2: Conditions of work and social protection
- Issue 3: Social dialogue
- Issue 4: Health and safety at work
- Issue 5: Human development and training in the workplace

Core Subject: The Environment
- Issue 1: Prevention of pollution
- Issue 2: Sustainable resource use
- Issue 3: Climate change mitigation and adaptation
- Issue 4: Protection of the environment, biodiversity, and restoration of natural habitats

Core Subject: Fair Operating Practices
- Issue 1: Anti-corruption
- Issue 2: Fair competition
- Issue 3: Promoting social responsibility in the value chain
- Issue 4: Respect for property rights

Core Subject: Consumer Issues
- Issue 1: Fair marketing, factual and unbiased information, and fair contractual practices
- Issue 2: Protecting consumers' health and safety
- Issue 3: Sustainable consumption
- Issue 4: Consumer service, support, and complaint and dispute resolution
- Issue 5: Consumer data protection and privacy
- Issue 6: Access to essential services
- Issue 7: Education and awareness

Core Subject: Community Involvement and Development
- Issue 1: Community involvement
- Issue 2: Education and culture
- Issue 3: Employment creation and skills development
- Issue 4: Technology development and access
- Issue 5: Wealth and income creation
- Issue 6: Health

7.3.2 *Social Justice and Community Development*

Social justice is a key topic in law, philosophy, social psychology, and education. Recently, researchers (e.g., Newell and Frynas, 2007; Rodrigo and Arenas, 2008) proposed using social justice, a system of fair relations between a firm and society, as a stringent assessment of a firm's CSR. From the social justice standpoint, CSR efforts can be categorised into at least two types: obligation- and development-based CSR efforts. Obligation-based CSR is defined by a host country's legal system and includes anti-corruption, tax obligations, product safety, labour rights, and so on. In other words, obligation-based CSR includes firms' 'fair' efforts towards other stakeholders in society. These efforts reflect how firms fairly treat their employees, consumers, and the environment.

Development-based CSR includes CSR activities that contribute to the development of the community; for foreign firms, the community refers to the host country. These include efforts to care for and enhance the development of the community. Going beyond legal requirements, development-based CSR aims to address the developmental needs of the community. For Chinese firms operating in a foreign country, these efforts are motivated by a sense of 'redistributing' the firm's wealth (redistribution justice) and co-evolving with the host nation. In emerging economies in particular, a Chinese firm's CSR efforts to educate the local staff and the community and to transfer technology and skills to improve employment and wealth are examples of such actions. Studies have shown that development-based CSR is more instrumental than obligation-based CSR in creating the goodwill to further a firm's performance in a host country (Tse, Hung, and Lwin, 2019). In African nations in particular, Chinese firms' efforts to aid in development have been highly valued.

7.3.3   Consumer Empowerment and Public Opinion

Over the past decade, China has transformed rapidly from a giant production house to a maturing consumer market. In addition to the government's role as a key driver of the CSR initiative, consumers are also becoming sensitised to the social impacts of firm activities. This is especially true for millennials, who frequently express their concerns regarding consumer rights and environmental protection online. Further, they often turn their concerns into actions, recommending brands that perform well in their CSR efforts to their friends and family, while punishing socially irresponsible brands by refusing to buy their products (Chu and Lin, 2012; Mouhamou, 2015). This situation is especially relevant to larger firms, which consumers may perceive as being 'greedy' while neglecting their social responsibilities.

By 2016, some Chinese consumers had begun making their collective voices public. This was made possible by the popularity of social media, which facilitates the diffusion of information online. They initiated nationwide surveys and later reported their lists of 'most hated brands' (Huanqui, 2016). This series of events highlights the fact that Chinese consumers have become key and active stakeholders, urging local and foreign firms in China to behave responsibly. Meanwhile, CSR offers an opportunity for firms to build consumers' brand trust and their relationship with consumers. As noted by Ellen Cheng, MSL's Asia practice group lead for corporate and brand citizenship based in Beijing, being a good corporate citizen is a strong differentiating factor for brands. Her point was noted in the 2011 KPMG China CSR Report (Mouhamou, 2015). Thus, engaging in CSR activities and thereby gaining consumer goodwill is becoming a strong incentive for Chinese firms to regulate their behaviours.

7.4   CHINESE MNC AS AN AVID ADOPTER

Given the governmental incentives and consumer sentiments, the majority of large Chinese firms have become avid adopters of CSR. Yet, many of them are at a crossroads, trying to transform their OEM operations into full-fledged MNC operations. Indeed, these fledging firms are faced with a pressing task during this stage of transforming their business model – the need to develop reputable, trust-inspiring brands. The extent to which Chinese firms have or have not been successful in this regard is reflected in their world rankings.

Although close to 100 Chinese MNCs are listed among the Fortune Global 500, only Huawei and Lenovo made Interbrand's list of the top 100 brands in 2017. Whereas these rankings reflect Chinese firms' substantial 'hard power' in gaining revenue and enlarging market shares, their achievements are diminished by their lack of 'soft power' in corporate reputation and brand management, in which CSR plays a salient role. A survey carried out by the global public relations firm Edelman substantiated these findings. Whereas Chinese MNCs enjoyed an 83 per cent trust rate in the domestic market, they had a much lower trust rate (50 per cent) in other emerging markets and only a 24 per cent trust rate in developed markets (Zheng, 2013). In other words, many Chinese MNCs fail to gain trust in the international community. Considerable work remains to be done to align the firm's business with the goodwill of the host communities, be they emerging or developed markets.

7.4.1   Chinese Firms in Emerging Economies

Among the emerging economies into which Chinese firms have expanded, African nations are among their top investment destinations. Indeed, since the founding of the People's Republic of China, the country has built strong social, economic, and diplomatic ties with African nations. Trade between China and Africa has grown exponentially since the 1990s; by 2009, China surpassed the USA to become Africa's largest trading partner (Sun and Rettig, 2014). Currently, Sino–African trade approaches USD300 billion annually, and the trade volume is likely to rise to USD400 billion by 2020 (Xinhua, 2015).

In spite of concerns over Chinese firms' expansion that may lead to social and environmental exploitation, as expressed in some news headlines, a study conducted by the Brookings Institute shows that China's direct investment in Africa is highly diverse (Chen, Dollar, and Tang, 2015). These Chinese MNCs invest and operate in both democratic and authoritarian regimes, and, contrary to popular views, Chinese investments in Africa are not concentrated in the extraction of natural resources. Rather, services comprise the most common sector, and there are also significant investments in manufacturing, especially in countries with an abundant workforce (Chen, Dollar, and Tang, 2015). These countries at the early stage of industrialisation are attracting investments in labour-intensive industries such as textiles, shoemaking, garments, and household appliances. Moreover, given its interest in diverse industries, China has contributed to infrastructure development, including highways, railways, telecommunications, and electric power, to facilitate regional connectivity in its trading nations. In return, Chinese firms pump in the technology and funds to assist these diverse developments. These projects are consistent with the firms' investment needs as well as the CSR objective to engage in community development. These initiatives that co-evolve with the host countries create a win–win situation for both firms and the host economies.

However, there have been numerous reports highlighting concerns over Chinese MNCs' business negotiations with local governments in Africa and other emerging economies. For example, the consortium led by China's Railway Construction Corp to build a high-speed rail in Mexico had its contract revoked amid a political scandal involving President Peña Nieto (Estevez, 2015). This and other alleged corruptive cases can seriously tarnish the image of a firm. There is a need for more transparency to the media and other stakeholders when firms negotiate with the local government (i.e., specific politicians and officers). Thus, conducting fair operating practices (i.e., anticorruption) remains an obligation that needs to be satisfied before development-based CSR can help boost the public's trust towards a firm and its legitimacy in a host market.

In the high-speed rail project in Pakistan, Power Construction Corporation of China hired 3,000 local workers and offered six months of free technical training in China to 100 Pakistani operation and maintenance workers (Lu, 2018). In Africa, similar initiatives have won strong local support. For example, the Mombasa–Nairobi Standard Gauge Railway improved Kenya's GDP by 1.5 per cent and provided 46,000 local jobs (Yamei, 2018).

In a recent CNN report on Chinese SMEs operating in Africa (Marsh, 2018), the CSR efforts by these SMEs were portrayed as more obligational than developmental. For example, a garment factory from Dongguan in Rwanda employed 10,000 workers with a survival-base entry pay. However, the salary of high-performance staff could be doubled. Since there is no minimal salary in Rwanda, this minimum compensation does not violate any established labour practice. In addition, the factory is hygienic and well managed. In this regard, the SMEs met the obligational CSR without any developmental CSR. This does not come as a surprise, since SMEs in the clothing industry are highly vulnerable to global price competition.

7.4.2   Chinese Firms in Developed Economies

As China is itself an emerging economy, the co-development approach that has worked well in emerging economies may not be appropriate in developed economies. Thus, Chinese MNCs adopt an alternative CSR model in developed economies. Huawei (USA), for example, emphasised that its supply chain was environmentally sustainable. This is in contrast to its co-development emphases in developing economies in Africa (e.g., Botswana) and in Pakistan, where student education and talent developments are emphasised (Huawei, 2017).

As discussed earlier, survey results show that most Chinese MNCs scored a low 24 per cent trust rate in developed economies. Thus, improving public perception would be an important task for Chinese firms to operate in these markets. One perspective is that the public's largely negative sentiments are 'normal', as emerging market MNCs (such as Chinese firms) represent a relatively new phenomenon and Chinese MNCs are at an early stage of development. This is the view taken by Wang Jianlin, chairman of Dalian Wanda Group Co. Ltd, a Chinese real-estate developer that has expanded aggressively overseas in recent years. Accordingly, Chinese firms need to invest time and effort to build a trusting relationship with the public in developed countries. CSR may provide a tool for these firms to ease into the host markets.

Nevertheless, a low level of trust presents a real challenge for Chinese firms in developed economies. There are several causes for a low trust level, including a low level of brand familiarity, a lack of transparency and openness in the firm's corporate culture, and sensitivities about state involvement in the host countries. Interestingly, consumer surveys indicated yet another basic cause: the perceived inferior quality of Chinese products (Zheng, 2013). Since producing quality products is a means to protect consumer health and safety, Chinese firms need to pursue this obligation-based CSR as a fundamental means to earn local market trust.

Meanwhile, Chinese firms can also take a proactive approach to pursue CSR activities. A survey conducted in the USA and the UK that examined the effects of localisation may shed light on this issue (Hung, 2015). Specifically, respondents indicated that localisation practices may enhance a Chinese firm's social legitimacy in these markets. More in-depth analyses indicated that some respondents harbour negative sentiments towards Chinese MNCs given their concern over the potential loss of jobs to China. This suggests that localisation may provide a means to pursue developmental CSR in developed markets. In sum, improving product quality and localisation are salient means to enhance developed host markets' acceptance of Chinese firms.

7.4.3 The Case of Huawei

Huawei is a global IT solution provider with a strong presence in Africa. It partners with most African countries, usually in smartphone distribution or in network infrastructure deployment. Huawei defines its CSR vision in Africa as 'growing with Africa', with the activities outlined in its corporate reports, CSR reports, and African CSR reports. Until 2005, when the Chinese government proposed the Harmonious Society Policy, Huawei's CSR activities took a traditional benefactor approach and included disaster relief, donations to education, and employee volunteers.

Beginning in 2006, the firm took a proactive approach in IT domain that aimed at building relationships and trust with the host countries through its CSR activities. The focus of this approach is co-development; that is, the firm aims to contribute to the development of local communities by 'bridging the digital divide'. Related activities include building telecommunication infrastructure, extending telecommunications services to remote areas, building training centres, and training local employees. Human resource development is perceived not only as a way to produce the much-needed local talent, but also as a way to contribute to local communities' sustainable development. In addition, it contributes to healthcare, education, and environmental conservation, all of which are activities in line with international standards of CSR practices.

Interestingly, Huawei also stressed the firm's own growth and economic contributions to the host country (revenues, profits, taxes paid). The latter focus is in line with China's approach to CSR, which stresses a firm's progress and economic contributions to society (Tang and Li, 2011). Also of interest is Huawei's portrayal of its workplace conditions, which can be in a hostile environment, given the geographic regions in which some of Huawei's operations are located. Rather than lamenting the difficulties or admitting the poor working conditions, Huawei stressed the determination, fighting spirit, and heroism of its staff. For example, it praised staff members who walked eight hours to provide the needed customer service as members that embodied the 'soul' of Huawei's culture (Tang and Li, 2011).

Huawei's approach to CSR in African countries is emulated by some other Chinese MNCs, including leading SOEs, in response to the negative image of Chinese firms and their disconnect from local communities. Firms such as Sinosteel, Sinopec, China Minmetals, and CNPC have begun to disclose publicly their social investment and impact in Africa through CSR reports. Thus, there is a dedicated effort to address and showcase sustainability activities in the emerging economies in which Chinese MNCs invest. Table 7.1 outlines some of the CSR projects Huawei carried out in developing and developed economies (Huawei, 2017).

7.5   CONCLUSION

When foreign MNCs introduced CSR practices to China in the mid-1990s, Chinese firms were reluctant to take up these initiatives. Since then, Chinese firms have made substantial improvements in this area. Engaging in CSR practices has become the norm among SOEs and large private firms over the past decade. The major driver for this change in firm attitudes and behaviour rests in the Chinese government, which it developed and adopted a set of CSR guidelines comparable to, and in some regards surpassing, international standards in 2016. The changing expectations among consumers, especially Internet-savvy young Chinese consumers, are also salient in this movement. Further, Chinese firms recognised over time the central role CSR may play in helping to correct the social and environmental problems in the country as well as enhancing their own competitiveness in the international arena. While Chinese firms are not forerunners in CSR, the major firms are quickly adopting some of the best practices.

Some CSR dimensions that are unique to Chinese society and culture, such as employment, social stability, and progress, are

Table 7.1 *Huawei's CSR projects in developing and developed economies*

Huawei's flagship CSR projects starting in 2008	
In developing economies	In developed economies
Hungary: Launched the Seeds for the Future programme to help train talented students in IT	**Germany**: Huawei Germany hosted 'Chinese 2.0', a new CSR project with the state government
Belarus: Sponsored the 'China Trip' essay and photography contest for teenagers on a rehabilitation trip from areas destroyed by the Chernobyl nuclear accident	**Denmark**: Launched the Seeds for the Future programme that contributes to Denmark's innovation and technology
Costa Rica: Participated in book donation hosted by the minister of culture	**Switzerland**: Successfully carried out the Global ICT programme to nurture IT talent
Panama: Signed a co-operation agreement with the New Generation Movement	**Spain**: Launched training programme 'El Futuro de las TIC'
Pakistan: Sponsored the Students Internship programme and offered job opportunities for interns after graduation	**USA**: Championed the 'K to College' School Supply programme to Stockton (California) Area Youth
Philippines: Participated in a CSR forum to strengthen CSR and sustainability leadership	**ALL**: Strengthened co-operation with customers, supplier and industry organisations to maintain sustainable supply chains
Kampuchea: Contributed to the IT industry and donations in Cambodia	
Kenya: Joined with UN High Commissioner for Refugees and Safaricom to provide tablets for refugees	
Zambia: Organised CSR charity events with the vice president of Zambia	

accentuated in the CSR guidelines in China. These dimensions have gained popular support and are duly practiced in China today. As Chinese firms continue to develop, they will likely improve and fine-tune their CSR efforts in China.

For the Chinese firms that operate in emerging economies, where co-development is highly appreciated, these firms are increasing involved in the host communities. In addition to obligation-based CSR efforts, the guidelines from the Chinese government help to encourage these firms to engage in development-based CSR efforts. As a result, the opportunities for Chinese firms in African nations will continue to prosper.

Chinese MNCs are still searching for an effective approach to earn the trust of consumers in developed economies. The recent survey findings show that, while CSR practices contribute to building trust, some consumption-related factors such as brand awareness and product quality are dominating the public's views. There are also sceptical and ethnocentric tendencies that need to be dissipated. Indeed, the survey findings further confirm that CSR is a form of 'soft power' that is useful in closing the 'trust gap' between Chinese firms and the public in developed economies.

REFERENCES

Bansal, P. (2005). Evolving sustainably: a longitudinal study of corporate sustainable development. *Strategic Management Journal*, 26(3): 197–218.

Chen, W., Dollar, D., and Tang, H. (2015). China's direct investment in Africa: reality versus myth. *Africa in Focus, Brookings.* 3 September. Retrieved 12 July 2019. www.brookings.edu/blogs/africa-in-focus/posts/2015/09/03-china-africa-investment-trade-myth-chen-dollar-tang.

Chu, S-C. and Lin, J.-S. (2012). Do Chinese consumers care about corporate social responsibility? *Asian Journal of Business Research*, 2(1): 69–91.

Cody, E. (2005). China warns gap between rich, poor is feeding unrest. *Washington Post.* 22 September. Retrieved 12 July 2019. www.washingtonpost.com/wp-dyn/content/article/2005/09/21/AR2005092100727.html.

CSR Asia and Embassy of Sweden. (2014). *A Study on Corporate Social Responsibility Development and Trends in China.* Retrieved 29 July 2019.

www.csr-asia.com/report/CSR-development-and-trends-in-China-FINAL-hires.pdf.

Donaldson, T. and Preston, L. E. (1995). The stakeholder theory of the corporation: concepts, evidence, and implications. *Academy of Management Review*, 20(1): 65–91.

Estevez, D. (2015). Mexico suspends multibillion dollar high-speed rail project at center of political scandal. *Forbes*. 10 February. Retrieved 12 July 2019. www.forbes.com/sites/doliaestevez/2015/02/10/mexico-suspends-multibillion-dollar-high-speed-rail-project-at-center-of-political-scandal/#13e0f57a2f12.

Fang, W. (2015). 'Corporate Social Responsibility Blue Book' (2015) published in Beijing. *Economic Information Daily*. 2 November. (方烨 (2015), 企业社会责任蓝皮书（2015）在京发布. 經濟參考, 11月2日.). Retrieved 12 July 2019. http://jjckb.xinhuanet.com/2015-11/02/c_134774246.htm.

Freeman, R. E. (1984). *Strategic Management: A Stakeholder Approach*. Cambridge: Cambridge University Press.

Hatton, C. (2015). Under the dome: the smog film taking China by storm. *BBC News*. 2 March. Retrieved 12 July 2019. www.bbc.com/news/blogs-china-blog-31689232.

Huanqui. (2016). Most hated foreign fast food brands in China. *Huanqui*. 14 March. Retrieved 29 July 2019. http://world.huanqiu.com/exclusive/2016-03/8697141.html?agt=15425.

Huawei. (2017). *2017 Sustainability Report*. Retrieved 12 July 2019. www-file.huawei.com/-/media/corporate/pdf/sustainability/2017-huawei-sustainability-report-en.pdf?la=en&source=corp_comm.

Hung, K. (2015). Gaining support in foreign markets: how effective are CSR practices? *International Conference on Research in Advertising (ICORIA), Flash Drive Proceedings*.

Hung, K., Tse, C. H., and Cheng, S. (2012). Advertising research in the post-WTO decade in China: meeting the internationalization challenge. *Journal of Advertising*, 41(Fall): 121–46.

Lu, Y. (2018). Chinese construction earns high reputation from overseas. *People's Daily*. 28 August. Retrieved 12 July 2019. www.newsghana.com.gh/chinese-construction-earns-high-reputation-from-overseas.

Marsh, J. (2018). By China. *CNN World*. Retrieved 12 July 2019. http://edition.cnn.com/interactive/2018/08/world/china-africa-ethiopia-manufacturing-jobs-intl.

Matten, D. and Moon, J. (2008). 'Implicit' and 'explicit' CSR: a conceptual framework for a comparative understanding of corporate social responsibility. *Academy of Management Review*, 33(2): 404–24.

Mitchell, R. K., Agle, B. R., and Wood, D. J. (1997). Toward a theory of stakeholder identification and salience: defining the principle of who and what really counts. *Academy of Management Review*, 22(4): 853–86.

Mouhamou, S. (2015). Corporate social responsibility in China: good for business is good for us. *The Nanjinger Magazine*. 19 October. Retrieved 12 July 2019. www .linkedin.com/pulse/corporate-social-responsibility-china-good-business-us- mouhamou.

Newell, P., and Frynas, J. G. (2007). Beyond CSR? Business, poverty and social justice: an introduction. *Third World Quarterly*, 28(4): 669–81.

Rodrigo, P., and Arenas, D. (2008). Do employees care about CSR programs? A typology of employees according to their attitudes. *Journal of Business Ethics*, 83(2), 265–83.

Sarkis, J., Ni, N., and Zhu, Q. (2011). Winds of change: corporate social responsibility in China. *Ivey Business Journal*. January/February. Retrieved 12 July 2019. https://iveybusinessjournal.com/publication/winds-of-change- corporate-social-responsibility-in-china.

Schmidpeter, R. and Stehr, C. (2015). 'A History of Research on CSR in China: The Obstacles for the Implementation of CSR in Emerging Markets'. In *Sustainable Development and CSR in China: A Multi-Perspective Approach*, R. Schmidpeter, H. Lu, C. Stehr, and H. Huang, eds. Zurich: Springer International Publishing.

Smith, J. (2012). The companies with the best CSR reputations. *Forbes*. 10 December. Retrieved 12 July 2019. www.forbes.com/sites/jacquelynsmith/2012/12/10/the- companies-with-the-best-csr-reputations/#58f99ceaa727.

Sun, Y. and Rettig, M. (2014). American and Chinese trade with Africa: rhetoric vs. reality. *The Hill*. 5 August. Retrieved 12 July 2019. http://thehill.com/blogs/ pundits-blog/international/214270-american-and-chinese-trade-with-africa -rhetoric-vs-reality.

Tang, L. and Li, H. (2011). 'Chinese Corporate Diplomacy: Huawei's CSR Discourse in Africa'. In *Soft power in China: Public Diplomacy through Communication*, J. Wang, ed. New York: Palgrave Macmillan, 95–115.

Tse, D.K., Hung, K., and Lwin, M.O. (2019). How obligatory, fair and developmental CSR affect corporate image and long-term goals of foreign firms in China. Unpublished paper.

Wang, J. and Chaudhri, V. (2009). Corporate social responsibility engagement and communication by Chinese companies. *Public Relations Review*, 35: 247–50.

Wang, L. and Juslin, H. (2009). The impact of Chinese culture on corporate social responsibility: the harmony approach. *Journal of Business Ethics*, 88: 433–51.

World Bank. (2007). *Cost of Pollution in China: Economic Estimates of Physical Damages*. Washington, DC: World Bank. Retrieved 12 July 2019. http://docu ments.worldbank.org/curated/en/2007/02/7503894/cost-pollution-china-eco nomic-estimates-physical-damages.

Xinhua. (2015). China–Africa trade approaches $300 billion in 2015. *China Daily*. 10 November. Retrieved 12 July 2019. www.chinadaily.com.cn/business/2015 -11/10/content_22417707.htm.

Xu, S. and Yang, R. (2010). Indigenous characteristics of Chinese corporate social responsibility conceptual paradigm. *Journal of Business Ethics*, 93: 321–33.

Yamei. (2018). Spotlight: China, Africa work to play concerto for shared future. *Xinhua*. 30 August. Retrieved 12 July 2019. www.xinhuanet.com/english/2018-08/30/c_137431296.htm.

Zheng, Y. (2013). China's global firms face 'trust gap'. *China Daily*. 12 September. Retrieved 12 July 2019. http://usa.chinadaily.com.cn/business/2013-09/12/con tent_16963073.htm.

8   Managing National Image

8.1 INTRODUCTION

Nation branding refers to a state government's extended efforts to mobilise multiple means to build, project and maintain a preferred national image in the international community. Seminal works by Anholt and others (Anholt, 2005; Nye, 2004) examined how nation-states could build and manage their images in an increasingly connected world, the complexity of which is heightened by global events and differential values in international relations (Nye, 2004). These developments have led different nations to engage in image cultivation so as to develop a competitive image over other nations (Szondi, 2008). The governmental efforts invested into nation branding are well spent, as countries with favourable images are in a better position to attract scarce resources to boost trade and investment, and attract tourism and talents in an increasingly competitive and resource-stringent world.

Aside from economic gains, a nation's image carries intangible benefits, as it influences what is said about the country in the media and how the message is interpreted by people around the world. Given their accessibility in the digital era, news reports on a country are salient contributors to the national brand. Through favourable reporting, a country with a good image may be excused for a seemingly unfortunate event or decision. Meanwhile, a country with a poor image may find the media reacting with indifference or cynicism even to its genuine humanitarian efforts (Anholt, 2005). Thus, a reputable, trusted image may act as a pre-emptive measure that guards a nation against potential fallout in the global media, which tends to oversimplify, often unfairly, complex issues in international affairs.

As an economic power, China has become increasingly preoccupied with its image as the country extends its global footprint. Over the past decade, considerable cultural, peacemaking, and diplomatic efforts have been made to promote the country as an attractive and trusted member of the international community. There are now more than 500 branches of the Confucius Institute to promote the Chinese language and culture on six continents. By contributing both finances and personnel in its operations, China has gained a leadership position in UN peacekeeping (Pauley, 2018). Moreover, China coordinated multilateral talks to ease diplomatic tensions and has hosted mega events such as the 2008 Olympics and the 2010 World Expo (Hung, 2015). These developments in public diplomacy have helped to project an image of China as a nation of 'peace, civilisation, and might' in the international arena (Pauley, 2018). Indeed, China enjoys a generally neutral to good image around the world. However, there are considerable variations in how it is perceived in different countries, an issue we will return to later in this chapter.

On the business front, the country's ascension to the WTO and the high-profile anti-graft campaign initiated by President Xi indicated the country's willingness to align structures and regulations of its business environment to international norms (Hung, Tse, and Cheng, 2012). Meanwhile, as Chinese firms and products go global, they inevitably project an image for the country, while, at the same time, they are affected by the national image in their firm operations and consumer buying decisions in the host countries.

This chapter examines the image of China from different perspectives: the general view, the view from its major trading partners, and the view from developing countries. The image of Chinese firms and products and the challenges they face will also be examined. The chapter will then discuss two advertising campaigns carried out by the Chinese government to manage the national image. In spite of its efforts, China has yet to project the intended country image among its national competitors.

8.2 BBC-GLOBESCAN RATING FOR CHINA

8.2.1 An Overview

The intense interests in nation branding around the world have prompted the development of professional benchmarks such as East Asia Institute's soft power index and the Anholt-GfK Roper Nation Brands Index to research and compare national images over time and across nations. Among these indices, the BBC-GlobeScan country-rating poll marks one of the most popular national image surveys, as findings of the polls are often reported in the media and are readily accessible on the Internet. Conducted almost annually since July 2004 (except 2015 and 2016), BBC-GlobeScan tracks the opinions of people in more than twenty countries regarding their impressions of various countries, including China. The longitudinal survey results have provided researchers with a perspective on how the world looks at China (and other surveyed countries) over the past thirteen years.

Figure 8.1 shows the world's perceptions of China from 2005 to 2017 (BBC World Service, 2005, 2006, 2007, 2008, 2009, 2010, 2011, 2012, 2013, 2014, 2017). The main question the survey asks is what influences a specific country has on the world. Respondents then indicate whether that country has a 'mainly positive' or 'mainly negative' influence (in addition to 'depends', 'neither/neutral', and 'N.A.'). The top two lines in Figure 8.1 show the percentage of respondents with 'mainly positive' or 'mainly negative' views towards China over the thirteen-year period. The bottom 'net' line shows the percentage difference between 'mainly positive' and 'mainly negative' views. The opinions of Chinese respondents were excluded. A subsample of respondents also indicates whether their impressions are influenced mainly by (1) the country's foreign policy; (2) tradition and culture, including arts, music, and food; (3) the way the country treats its people; or (4) its economy, products, and services.

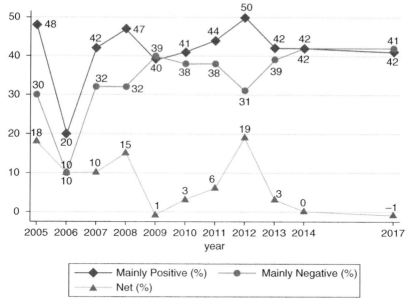

FIGURE 8.1 World perception of China: percentage of people holding mainly positive or negative views on China
Source: BBC World Service (2005, 2006, 2007, 2008, 2009, 2010, 2011, 2012, 2013, 2014, 2017)

The figure shows a positive net rating for China in eight of the eleven surveys conducted over the past thirteen years, indicating that, on average, respondents held more positive than negative views of the country. Doug Miller, then-president of GlobeScan, suggested that respondents attributed the high net rating from 2005 (18 per cent) to China's 'exceptional economic achievement'. This rating showed that China was viewed as playing a significantly more positive role in the world than either the USA (-18 per cent) or Russia (-48 per cent), the superpowers of the Cold War. Unfortunately, there has since been a downward trend, with China's national image dipping from a net rating of 18 per cent in 2005 to -1 per cent in 2017. Interestingly, in spite of the unfavourable trend, China still maintains a significantly more positive image than either the USA (-15 per cent) or Russia

(-20 per cent). Perhaps the international community in general is not fond of superpowers. In addition to revealing the general trend, the polls also indicated irregularities in the years 2009 (net rating = -1 per cent), 2012 (net rating = 19 per cent), and 2013 (net rating = 3 per cent). We will discuss these particular years in more details in the following sections.

Consistent with the emphasis China has placed on its economic role in the world, respondents cited the country's 'economy, products, and services' as the main drivers for their perceptions of the country. The one time China scored higher than the initial 18 per cent was in 2012 (19 per cent), when the significant improvement over the previous year was attributed by the respondents to China's strong and robust economy. GlobeScan's president Chris Coulter commented, 'The turmoil in the EU, long seen as an attractive bastion of political and economic stability, has raised doubts in people's minds about its continued ability to be a global leader. Hopes are turning to China.' However, the high hope placed on China's economic performance is a double-edged sword. When its economy slowed down in 2009 (2008: 18.1 per cent; 2009: 8.6 per cent), the country's net ratings dropped drastically when compared with previous years.

8.2.2 The Year 2013 and Beyond

In 2013, the BBC-GlobeScan survey again showed a drastic drop in the world's perception of China compared with the previous year. The strong deterioration of perceptions was especially marked in European and North American countries, indicating that Sino-political views may play an important role in the public's perceptions. Polls at Pew Research Center's Global Attitudes Project also showed a similar drop in China's favourability in the USA and Western Europe around this time. According to Pew Research, the 2011–13 net change in favourable attitudes towards China dropped 14 per cent in the USA, 11 per cent in the UK, 9 per cent in France, and 6 per cent in Germany (Pew Research Center, 2013).

The drop in China's favourability in the Western world has been attributed to several factors, including China's growing economic power, the unease in the Western world about China as a commercial competitor, and European frustration with China's insistence on treating, for example, Hong Kong, as an "internal affair". In the USA, there is growing concern about the country's trade deficit with China as well as the substantial Chinese holding of US debt that could potentially be used by China as bargaining chips. More recently, there has been growing public concern regarding Chinese companies buying American assets. Although these deals remain rare, the size of the deals is growing. The USD10.5 billion spent by Chinese companies in 2013 to purchase American companies nearly doubled the USD5.3 billion worth of deals in 2012. The 2012 figure was, in turn, well above the USD863.6 million spent in 2011 for the same purpose (Davidson and Weise, 2013).

8.2.3 American Views on China

Aside from the world's views in general, the perceptions of people residing in countries with significant links to China are of particular interest. As China is known as the 'world factory', its image among major trading partners such as the USA deserves serious attention. Not only would an unfavourable image affect China's exports, unfavourable public opinions may also exert pressure on the US government to tighten its trade policies towards China.

Figure 8.2 outlines Americans' views on China during the past decade (BBC World Service, 2005, 2006, 2007, 2008, 2009, 2010, 2011, 2012, 2013, 2014, 2017). Unlike worldviews on China, American perceptions have remained consistently negative. In particular, the years 2008–10 indicated an especially low point in American perceptions. This reflects a trend that started in 2007, when a series of large-scale recalls on Chinese-made products erupted. These recalls ranged from pet food to tyres and toys (e.g., Mattel) and raised people's concerns over the quality and safety of products made in China.

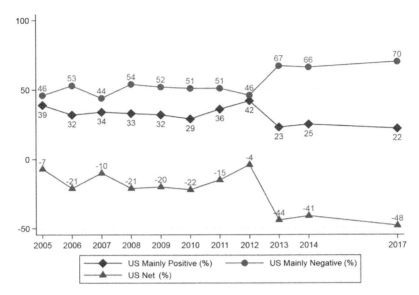

FIGURE 8.2 US perception of China: percentage of Americans holding
mainly positive or negative views on China
Source: BBC World Service (2006, 2007, 2008, 2009, 2010, 2011, 2014),
Digital Repository at the University of Maryland (2005), Globescan (2012,
2013, 2017)

Furthermore, the year 2013 brought an even more drastic drop in
American views on China, which have not recovered to date. Similar
to Western Europeans, Americans are becoming concerned with
China's growing economic power and especially Chinese
firms' M&A activities. Although Chinese firms have bought global
assets such as oil, iron ore, and other commodities in the past to feed
its industrial needs, these acquisitions were, in general, far from the
American public's scrutiny. However, Shuanghui Group's 2013 proposed buyout of Virginia-based Smithfield Foods Inc., the world's
largest pork and hog producer, was closer to home for American consumers. Some expressed concern over China's food safety record and
the potential effect on their health, in spite of the company's reassur-
ance that pork would be exported to China rather than imported to the
USA. Others wondered if food should be taken as a strategic defence

item and called on the US government to stop the deals that could infringe on national security (Kitchen, 2013).

As Chinese firms broaden their investment scope globally, their moves will likely involve an ever wider array of industries. In an interconnected world where politics, business moves, and public sentiment interplay with one another, some of these moves may cause public unease in host markets. We posit that national image concerns need to be taken into serious consideration as Chinese firms globalise their operations.

8.2.4 Developing Countries' Views on China

Contrary to the negative views expressed by respondents in Western countries, the BBC-GlobeScan surveys consistently showed more positive views on China from developing countries, especially those in the sub-Saharan region. Indeed, in spite of an across-the-board drop in net ratings for China in 2013, countries such as Pakistan (75 per cent), Nigeria (68 per cent), Ghana (47 per cent), and Egypt (46 per cent) continued to give China very high net ratings. After all, China has made a dramatic rise in a few decades, transforming from one of the world's poorest countries into an economic power, while also reducing poverty and illiteracy and increasing the lifespan of its citizens. For a developing country facing domestic poverty and its many ills, China offers a realistic and reachable model to emulate.

Since different survey instruments may yield different results given the questions asked and the countries surveyed, we cross-validated the finding of the BBC-GlobeScan with the results of the China National Image Global Survey. With data collected annually from 2013 onwards, findings of the surveys concurred, indicating a wide disparity between developing and developed countries' perceptions of China, with developing countries consistently giving more positive ratings.

Table 8.1 lists selected findings of the China National Image Global Survey of 2016–17. As indicated in the table, respondents' overall impression of China in developing countries (6.9) is higher

Table 8.1 *Perceptual gap in China's National Image*

	Developing countries	Developed countries
• What is your overall impression of China? (ten-point scale)	6.9	5.6
• China's performance in science and technology (% thought highly)	76	55
• China's performance in the economy (% thought highly)	74	55
• Expectation of China's role in BRICS (% of high and relatively high expectations)	66	53
• Economic and trade co-operation between China and my country (% of those who would welcome more)	71	55
• Technological co-operation between China and my country (% of those would welcome more)	72	51
• What factors below would hold you back from choosing Chinese brands? (% indicating low quality)	62	63

Source: China National Image Global Survey (2017)

than that in developed countries (5.6, on a ten-point scales). Also of interest are the divided views on China's performance in the economy (developing: 74 per cent; developed: 55 per cent) and in science and technology (developing: 76 per cent; developed: 55 per cent). Again, developing countries provided higher ratings in these areas. The perceptual gap between developing/developed countries on China's achievements may indirectly reflect China's relevance to their respective national interests: developing countries attributed more highly China's role in BRIC (Brazil, Russia, India, and China) countries (developing: 66 per cent; developed: 53 per cent) and were looking for more economic (developing: 71 per cent; developed: 55 per cent) and technological co-operation (developing: 72 per cent; developed: 51 per cent) with China. To many developing countries, working with China may help bring jobs, infrastructure and investment that may be difficult to come by otherwise. Unfortunately, in both developing (62 per cent) and developed countries (63 per cent), low product quality remains a concern. Since products made in China comprise the third most important channel for overseas respondents to learn about China (after local traditional and new media), this is an area that requires serious attention if China wants to build and manage a favourable national image in the international community.

8.2.5   China–Africa Trading Relationship

Various longitudinal surveys have shown that African nations consistently give favourable ratings to China. Indeed, China's special bond with African nations can be traced back to the 1950s and 1960s, when the latter struggled for self-determination and independence. This special bond was consolidated in the 1970s, when China, then a poor nation, helped built the USD500 million Tanzania–Zambia Railway (TAZARA) through some of Africa's most rugged terrain. The TAZARA became an enduring symbol of the solidarity among developing nations in general. This megaproject was also emblematic of Chinese support for African development.

Although the investments during the following decades were low, Chinese investments in Africa have soared over the past two decades, and by 2009 China became the African continent's largest trading partner. Given the paucity of quality data, there is a great deal of misunderstanding of the China–Africa trading relationship in the developed world. In particular, China's investments and co-operation projects in Africa have often been criticised by Western politicians and media as neocolonial abuses that could lead to debt crises and the loss of natural resources on the continent. This viewpoint can be contrasted with the optimism and highly positive image attributed to

China by many African people (e.g., in BBC-GlobeScan surveys), who regard the partnership with China as a 'brotherhood' (Van Mead, 2018).

To make sense of the diverse viewpoints, two comprehensive sources released in 2016 and 2017, respectively, may shed light into the China–Africa trading relationship. The first is an exclusive database on Chinese loans to Africa (2000–14) compiled by the China–Africa Research Initiative (CARI) at Johns Hopkins University. The other is a McKinsey & Company study on China's business engagement in eight African countries. Eom (2016) compared different databases on Chinese loans to Africa and found that the Johns Hopkins database was well-supported across multiple sources. By contrast, some previously reported databases (e.g., Rand Corporation, AidData, Ritch Ratings) have serious errors and significantly overstated the number and value of Chinese loans, such that observers and researchers alike may have reached inaccurate conclusions.

Analysis of the Johns Hopkins database showed that Chinese loans to Africa focus primarily on building connective infrastructures in transportation (e.g., roads, railroads), communication (e.g., mobile technology), and energy (e.g., electrical plant, wind farm). This emphasis on infrastructure coincided with the African Union's thirty-year strategy to prioritise the building of regional and continental infrastructure needed to further African development and improve Africa's economy. The Chinese loans were provided to a cross-section of African nations with few political strings attached (except for the recognition of the One China policy). Whereas resource-rich Angola was the top recipient of Chinese loans, resource-poor Ethiopia also benefitted as the next in line. Almost 90 per cent of the Ethiopian loans went to building roads, railways, and power lines to improve the country's accessibility (Eom, 2016).

Aside from engaging in infrastructure projects, Chinese firms in Africa operate in diverse industry sectors, including manufacturing, services, trading, and real estate (Sun, Jayaram, and Kassiri, 2017) to meet the continent's industrialisation and urbanisation challenges. Chinese firms also provided economic benefits to the host countries by providing jobs and transferring skills and technology. Among more than 1,000 Chinese firms and factories interviewed by McKinsey (2017), 89 per cent of the employees were African, including highly skilled workers and managers, thus disputing the myth that Chinese firms do not employ locals. Also, nearly two-thirds of the firms provided skills training and one-third introduced at least one new technology. In some cases, the improved technology together with the efficiencies of scale helped lower prices for existing products and services by as much as 40 per cent, thereby improving the quality of life of the locals (Sun, Jayaram, and Kassiri, 2017). Overall, Chinese investments and firm activities address the real developmental needs in many African nations (Eom, 2016).

The goodwill African nationals extend to China may reflect the improvements to their everyday life made possible by Chinese investments, loans, and firm activities, as well as their positive attitudes towards the locals. Further, the goodwill may include elements of hope as China's developmental path over the past few decades inspires African nationals to 'aspire towards the developmental state' (Kitaba, 2017). Nevertheless, the Chinese loans are huge at USD95.5 billion. 'The risk for African borrowers relates to the project's profitability,' says CARI Director Deborah Bräutigam (Van Mead, 2018). Nevertheless, given the optimism on both sides (Sun, Jayaram and Kassiri, 2017), there is high hope that the Chinese loans may produce a win–win situation to both the lenders and borrowers.

8.3 AD CAMPAIGN AS A PROMOTER OF CHINA'S NATIONAL IMAGE

Advertising is used by various countries to help project a preferred national image. Aside from promoting a country as a preferred tourist destination, some countries use advertising to project specific traits of their national culture to achieve a broader political objective. For example both Saudi Arabia (Zhang and Benoit, 2004) and the USA carried out image restoration ad campaigns in the post-9/11 era. The US campaign, in particular, targeted Middle Eastern countries to project the image of a harmonious, multi-cultural America that included the Muslim community (Kendrick and Fullerton, 2004).

China has taken strides over the past decade to use advertising to promote its national image abroad. In the following sections, we discuss two cases in which the Chinese government used outdoor (and online) advertising to manage the national image. The 'made-with-China' ad used a factual approach to encourage viewers to engage in reflective thinking about Chinese-made products. The 'experience China' ad, on the other hand, used an emotional approach to project the image of a modern China. The target viewers in both campaigns included the American public, whose views on China are not positive (e.g., in BBC-GlobeScan surveys). These case studies illustrate both potential successes and shortcomings in using advertising to cultivate China's national image.

8.3.1   Case 1: Changing Stereotypes on Chinese Exports

Products made in China suffered from a confidence crisis in 2007–9, when a series of product recalls and import bans were imposed by multiple countries, including the USA, Canada, the EU, Australia, and New Zealand. A content analysis of the *New York Times* indicated that during 2006–9, only 23 per cent of its reports on 'made in China' products were positive. This is a drastic drop from 46 per cent identified in an earlier study (Yin, 2014). Indeed, China's Nation Index for Products dipped from twenty-fourth place in 2005 to forty-seventh place in 2008, making it the third lowest ranking country on the index for that year (Anholt, 2010).

It was against this background that China's Ministry of Commerce commissioned an advertising campaign in 2009 in an attempt to reverse the negative perception of Chinese-made products in developed countries. The campaign, masterminded by ad agency DDB Guoan, was titled 'Made in China, Made with the World' (hereinafter the made-with-China ad). The thirty-second ad showcased five products embedded in different, yet typical, consumption situations among consumers in a developed country (the presumed target viewers). The products were purported to be made in China with 'American sports technology' (footwear); 'European styling' (refrigerator); 'software from Silicon Valley' (MP3 player); 'French designers' (dress); and 'engineers from all over the world' (aeroplane). Interested readers can view the ad on this link: www.youtube.com/watch?v=MINYux3mPUI.

Conceptually, the ad aimed at replacing the '100 per cent made-in-China' image with a composite 'made-with-country' image. The message also carries a positive connotation of China working 'with' other countries to produce the final product. These two effects were intended to reduce negative stereotypes, engage the viewers to reconsider the composition of 'made-in-China' products, and improve the global image of Chinese exports (Hung, 2015). The ad was aired in late 2009 on television networks among China's major trading partners, including CNN in the USA (for a six-week period) and the ad was also uploaded to the BBC website in the UK (for a five-week period).

Intrigued by this sequence of events, the authors conducted an original study to gauge the effectiveness of this ad. Specifically, the study adopted the reflective and impulsive model (Strack and Deutsch, 2004) as the theoretical framework to access how stereotyping could be changed by communicational means to manage a country's national image. The reflective and impulsive model posits that human behaviour is largely controlled by two interacting systems: impulsive and reflective responses. Impulsive responses are fast, spontaneous, and stereotype-based responses. Reflective responses, on the other hand, are represented by a person's rational thoughts. Results of the study would identify the extent the ad could induce reflective thoughts in the viewers and dampen some of their impulsive stereotype-based negative responses regarding the image of products made in China.

8.3.2   Effectiveness of the Made-with-China Ad

The authors' study was conducted using an online survey of 801 respondents in the USA (n = 389) and the UK (n = 412) (Hung, 2015).

Results showed that the ad was able to convey the main message reasonably well, although the effects were not very strong. The respondents thought that the products in the ad were global (3.54 out of a maximum of 5), and they were predisposed to try them (3.22 out of 5). We conducted additional analyses to identify the effects of impulsive responses (positive and negative emotions) and reflective responses (i.e., 'the ad makes me think differently about products made in China') on the viewers' buying intention towards Chinese-made products. Analysis results showed that viewers who reflected on the ad message (i.e., thought differently about products made in China after watching the ad) had stronger buying intention. Interestingly, the reflective thoughts also reduced the effects elicited by impulsive responses alone. Thus, the ad was able to (1) regulate viewers' stereotypes, (2) induce them to reconsider the meanings behind the made-in-China label, and (3) reconsider their buying intention towards Chinese exports. The findings were consistent across the US and UK samples.

In addition to the positive findings identified from our survey, Yin's (2014) longitudinal content analysis of the *New York Times* showed that, in the year following the airing of this ad, 100 per cent of the news reported in the *New York Times* on 'made in China' was positive, a drastic improvement from 23 per cent in the earlier period. Thus, the results of the Hung (2015) and Yin (2014) studies concurred. The 'made with China' ad exerted positive effects in the USA, the targeted country. Whereas the quality of Chinese exports is but one of the aspects people consider when they think of the image of China, GlobeScan results showed that the perceptions of China in the eyes of the world and among Americans improved in 2010 and beyond.

8.3.3   Case 2: The 'Experience China' Ad

A year after airing the 'made with China' ad, the Chinese government embarked on another ad campaign to promote its country image. This campaign coincided with former President Hu Jintao's state visit to the USA in January 2011. The sixty-second 'experience China' ad was featured at New York's Times Square. A shorter thirty-second version followed and was aired on CNN for a month. Interested readers can refer to this link to view the ad: www.youtube.com/watch?v=570LHTMWoMw.

The 'experience China' ad featured fifty mainland Chinese celebrities and business leaders, including NBA superstar Yao Ming, pianist Lang Lang, astronaut Yang Liwei, and Alibaba CEO Ma Yun, as well as several ordinary Chinese people. According to Wang Lijun, senior executive of at the agency Shanghai Lowe & Partners that produced the ad, the celebrities 'represent the optimistic, upwardly mobile spirit of contemporary China'. The ad ended with a message of 'Chinese friendship' to indicate the willingness of these and other Chinese people to befriend people in other nations.

The 'experience China' ad received both positive and negative responses from American viewers. On the positive side, viewers indicated that the ad prompted their interest in China and its people, making them want to know more about the featured celebrities and their stories. On the negative side, some commentators questioned the high frequency at which the ad was shown (i.e., 300 times daily at Times Square). Others questioned the relevance of its contents to the American public, especially at a time when they were suffering from the aftermath of the financial crisis (Xu, 2014). David Wolf of the Wolf Group Asia lamented, 'With these ads, China probably hoped to open its arms to the American people. Instead ... it gave them the finger.' Nevertheless, Tom Dotoroff, CEO of J. Walter Thompson Asia-Pacific, considered the ad an important step in China's public diplomacy efforts (Chao, 2011).

8.3.4 An Illustrative Field Study on Promoting China's National Image

To provide a better understanding of the effects of this ad among viewers in different countries, including American viewers, we conducted an original online survey. The study examined viewer responses in four countries, including both developed countries (USA and UK) and developing countries (India and Malaysia) Hung (2019). The survey respondents were recruited from Millward Brown's e-panel. Four hundred respondents participated in each country (except Malaysia with 200 respondents). They included men and women across different age groups and income brackets.

Respondents were asked to select from a list the impressions they formed while viewing the ad. They could select one, more than one, or none of the provided phrases regarding their impression of the Chinese people. Interestingly, the percentage of respondents in each country who considered the Chinese people 'talented' or 'confident' outweighted the percentage who considered them 'friendly'. Thus, the ad successfully communicated the image of an 'optimistic, upwardly mobile' China as envisioned by the ad producer; however, the 'friendly' image, which was another important component of the ad message, was less successfully communicated (see Figure 8.3). The percentage of viewers who indicated that 'there are lots of talented people in China' was considerably lower in India (15 per cent) than in the remaining countries (24–6 per cent). As both India and China are emergent economies in Asia as well as members of the BRIC group, Indian viewers could potentially consider China a competitor economically and thereby might be less likely to form an impression of Chinese people as 'talented'.

Regarding the emotions elicited by the ad, the survey findings showed considerable differences between developed/Western countries (USA, UK) and developing/Asian countries (India, Malaysia). Asian viewers' responses were considerably more emotionally charged, with the ad eliciting higher percentages of *both* positive and negative emotions (see Figure 8.4). For example, more than 50 per cent of Asian viewers felt 'excited' viewing the ad (India: 57 per cent; Malaysia: 56 per cent) compared to just over 20 per cent of Western viewers (UK: 22 per cent; USA: 21 per cent). In addition, 70 per cent of Asian viewers felt 'inspired' (India: 70 per cent; Malaysia: 71 per cent) compared to just under 40 per cent of Western viewers (UK: 39 per cent; USA: 37 per cent). The negative emotions showed a similar divide between Asian and Western viewers. There were

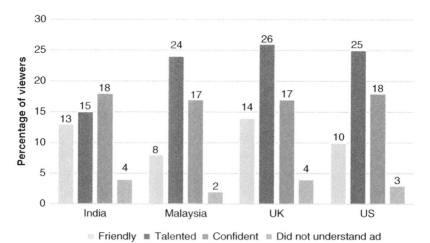

FIGURE 8.3 Viewer perception of 'experience China' ad
Source: Hung (2019)

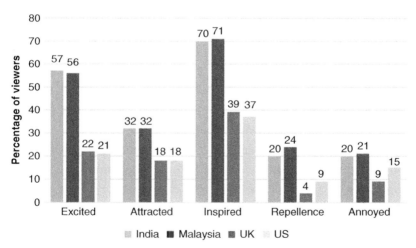

FIGURE 8.4 Viewers' emotional responses to 'experience China' ad
Source: Hung (2019)

more Asian viewers who felt 'repellence' (India: 20 per cent; Malaysia: 24 per cent) and 'annoyed' (India: 20 per cent; Malaysia: 21 per cent) than Western viewers (repellence: UK, 4 per cent, USA, 9 per cent;

annoyed: UK, 9 per cent, USA, 15 per cent). These findings implied once again that the views towards China and its people among geographically neighbouring countries were highly complex.

8.3.5   Beyond Ad Campaigns

As indicated in the previous sections, both campaigns achieved some levels of success in projecting the primary messages (i.e., Chinese-made products are sourced from many countries; there are talented people in China). However, neither campaign seemed to be successful in projecting the secondary message, intended to extend friendship to other nations ('working with [country X]' in ad 1 and 'Chinese friendship' in ad 2). Thus, the challenge remains of how Chinese national image ads can better improve mutual understanding and respect in the international community.

Recent efforts in promoting China's national image followed a multi-thong approach. In a televised interview on managing China's image (TVB, 2018), Professor Shi Anbin at Tsinghua University suggested that national image campaigns could be carried out by NGO or private firms to reduce governmental involvement. Relatedly, he suggested that the Confucius Institute could consider financing through a foundation to alleviate the concern raised in some Western countries that it was a governmental agency.

In addition to reducing the governmental involvement in national image campaigns, recent efforts were aimed at getting closer to the targeted viewers. Rather than using a big splash approach and overwhelming the viewers (e.g., featuring fifty people in the 'experience China' ad), national image campaigns should carry subtle messages that match the viewers' knowledge of and interests in China to garner the intended responses. For example, a campaign that promoted Chengdu (home to pandas) in the UK in 2012 featured 108 dancers dressed-up as pandas. They performed flash dances in public areas and offered 'bear hugs' to passers-by. Judging from the passers-by's responses, the campaign was well-received (TVB, 2018).

8.4 CONCLUSION

Bolstered by its strong economic growth over the past decades, China enjoys a neutral to good national image around the world. Its image is especially favourable during financial crises, when people around the world look to China to help rebuild the world economy. However, as China's economy has improved further to become a superpower in recent years, its image begins to suffer. This is especially an issue with the USA, its major trading partner, where China's national image has dropped to a record low in recent years amid trade tensions. The USA's unfavourable attitude towards China also reflects its growing concern over Chinese firms' M&A activities affecting American industries and firms. Meanwhile, there is a strong divide between the views of developed and developing countries towards China. Developing countries in general, and African countries in particular, hold positive views towards China. The latter is likely a result of China's no-strings-attached loans and investments to help build the much needed infrastructure on the African continent in terms of transportation, communication, and energy. Beyond infrastructure, investments by Chinese firms are now moving on to manufacturing, trading, and services that provide jobs, transfer skills, and technology to improve the living standard among people in host African countries.

To bolster its image, China has carried out advertising campaigns to attempt to improve its national image in developed countries, especially in the USA. These advertising attempts have two implications. First and foremost, the two campaigns proved to be effective in loosening some negative stereotypes about China. By stimulating reflective thought, the ads were able to counterbalance some impulsive (and negative) responses to the country. Second, while the two attempts achieved some positive results, the challenge remains high. Indeed, the global community is looking for evidence that China's rise to become a world leader is non-threatening to current leading countries of the world. This challenge is especially strong among the American public.

REFERENCES

Anholt, S. (2005). Anholt nation brands index: how does the world see America? *Journal of Advertising Research*, 45 (September): 296–304.

Anholt, S. (2010). *Places: Identity, Image and Reputation*. New York: Palgrave MacMillan.

BBC World Service. (2006). Global poll. Retrieved 29 July 2019. www.bbc.co.uk /pressoffice/pressreleases/stories/2006/02_february/03/poll.shtml.

BBC World Service. (2007). Israel and Iran share most negative ratings in global poll. Retrieved 29 July 2019. http://news.bbc.co.uk/2/shared/bsp/hi/pdfs/06_03_07 _perceptions.pdf.

BBC World Service. (2008). Global views of USA improve. Retrieved 29 July 2019. http://news.bbc.co.uk/2/shared/bsp/hi/pdfs/02_04_08_globalview.pdf.

BBC World Service. (2009). Views of China and Russia decline in global poll. Retrieved 29 July 2019. http://news.bbc.co.uk/2/shared/bsp/hi/pdfs/06_02_09 bbcworldservicepoll.pdf.

BBC World Service. (2010). Global views of United States improve while other countries decline. Retrieved 29 July 2019. http://news.bbc.co.uk/2/shared/bs p/hi/pdfs/160410bbcwspoll.pdf.

BBC World Service. (2011). Positive views of Brazil on the rise in 2011 BBC country rating poll. Retrieved 29 July 2019. www.bbc.co.uk/pressoffice/press releases/stories/2011/03_march/07/poll.pdf.

BBC World Service. (2014). Negative views of Russia on the rise: global poll. Retrieved 29 July 2019. https://downloads.bbc.co.uk/mediacentre/country-rating-poll.pdf.

Chao, L. (2011). Pro-China ad debuts in Times Square. *Wall Street Journal*. 18 January. Retrieved 15 July 2019. http://blogs.wsj.com/metropolis/2011/01/ 18/pro-china-ad-debuts-in-times-square/.

China National Image Global Survey. (2017). 2016–2017 China National Image Global Survey. Retrieved 29 July 2019. https://cn-en.kantar.com/business/bra nds/2018/2016-2017-china-national-image-global-survey/.

Davidson, P. and Weise, E. (2013). China's Shuanghui in $4.7B deal for Smithfield. *USA Today*. 29 May. Retrieved 15 July 2019. www.usatoday.com/story/money/ business/2013/05/29/smithfield-foods-china-acquisition/2368671COMP: link/.

Digital Repository at the University of Maryland. (2005). 23 national poll: who will lead the world? Retrieved 29 July 2019. https://drum.lib.umd.edu/bitstream/h

andle/1903/10667/LeadWorld_Apr05_art.pdf;jsessionid=34F9692B7FFBE32A2
D600B97D20AA39F?sequence=2.

Eom, J. (2016). 'China Inc.' becomes China the builder in Africa. *The Diplomat*.
29 September. Retrieved 15 July 2019. https://thediplomat.com/2016/09/china-
inc-becomes-china-the-builder-in-africa/.

Globescan. (2012). Views of Europe slide sharply in global poll, while views of
China improve. Retrieved 29 July 2019. https://globescan.com/images/ima
ges/pressreleases/bbc2012_country_ratings/2012_bbc_country%20rating%20f
inal%20080512.pdf.

Globescan. (2013). Views of China and India slide while UK's ratings climb: global
poll. Retrieved 29 July 2019. https://globescan.com/wp-content/uploads/2013/
05/2013_country_rating_poll_bbc_globescan.pdf.

Globescan. (2017). Fake Internet content a high concern, but appetite for regulation
weakens. Retrieved 29 July 2019. https://globescan.com/tag/bbc-world-service-
survey/.

Hung, K. (2015). 'Repairing the Made-in-China Image in the US and UK: Effects of
Government-Supported Advertising'. In *International Public Relations and
Public Diplomacy: Communication and Engagement*, G. Golan, S.-U. Yang,
and D. Kinsey, eds. New York: Peter Lang Publishing, 209–28.

Hung, K. (2019). Experience China ad: Perceptions across four countries. Working
paper.

Hung, K., Tse, C. H., and Cheng, S. (2012). Advertising research in the post-WTO
decade in China: meeting the internationalization challenge. *Journal of
Advertising*, 41(fall): 121–46.

Kendrick, A. and Fullerton, J. (2004). Advertising as public diplomacy: attitude
change among international audiences. *Journal of Advertising Research*, 44
(September): 297–311.

Kitaba, M. (2017). Why African nations welcome China. *The Diplomat*.
16 February. Retrieved 15 July 2019. http://thediplomat.com/2017/02/why-
african-nations-welcome-china/.

Kitchen, M. (2013). What will China buy? Beijing goes shopping in the US.
Retrieved 29 July 2019. www.marketwatch.com/story/what-will-china-buy-
beijing-goes-shopping-in-us-1383013399/.

Nye, J. (2004). *Soft Power*. New York: Public Affairs.

Pauley, L. (2018). China takes the lead in UN peacekeeping. *The Diplomat*.
17 April. Retrieved 15 July 2019. https://thediplomat.com/2018/04/china-
takes-the-lead-in-un-peacekeeping/.

Pew Research Center. (2013). America's global image remains more
positive than China's. *Pew Research Center*. 18 July. Retrieved 15 July 2019.

www.pewresearch.org/global/2013/07/18/americas-global-image-remains-more-positive-than-chinas/.

Strack, F. and Deutsch, R. (2004). Reflective and impulsive determinants of social behavior. *Personality and Social Psychology Review*, 8(3): 220–47.

Sun, I. Y., Jayaram, K., and Kassiri, O. (2017). *Dance of the Lions and Dragons: How Are Africa and China Engaging, and How Will the Partnership Evolve?* New York: McKinsey & Company.

Szondi, G. (2008). 'Public Diplomacy and Nation Branding: Conceptual Similarities and Differences'. In *Discussion Papers in Diplomacy*, V. Duthoit and E. Huijgh, eds. The Hague: Netherlands Institute of International Relations 'Clingendael'.

TVB (2018). 40 years of reform and opening up: image engineering. *TVB*. 11 November. Retrieved 29 July 2019. https://cs.mytvsuper.com/tc/login?destUrl=http%3A%2F%2Fwww.mytvsuper.com%2Ftc%2Fhome%2Fcp_highlightscp%2F40yearsofreforms_118425%2F405356%3Fentry%3Dseo.

Van Mead, N. (2018). China in Africa: win–win development, or a new colonialism? *The Guardian*. 31 July. Retrieved 15 July 2019. www.theguardian.com/cities/2018/jul/31/china-in-africa-win-win-development-or-a-new-colonialism.

Xu, H. (2014). 中国国家形象广告在美传播效果 [The communication effects of china national film in the U.S.]. *PR View*, 10: 38–48.

Yin, Y. (2014). 国家广告的推出–'携手中国制造"广告解析' [An analysis on 'made-with-China' ad]. *PR View*, 10: 13–22.

Zhang, J. and Benoit, W. L. (2004). Message strategies of Saudi Arabia's image restoration campaign after 9/11. *Public Relations Review*, 30(2): 161–7.

9 China's Technological Competence, Trade Relations, and Economic Co-operation

9.1 INTRODUCTION

Going beyond our discussion on the footprints, processes, failures, and challenges involved in how Chinese firms globalise their operations, this chapter takes a forward-looking view. It assesses the future of Chinese firms in the globalising economy, a topic that has been met with increased attention. This chapter conceptually assesses Chinese firms' future on the Chinese government's performance in three domains; namely, the nation's technological competence, its trade relations, and plan of co-operation with other nations. These domains are key elements of the institutional framework that will determine how Chinese firms fare in the global economy.

The first part of the chapter focuses on the technological domain, examining China's pool of technological talents (STEM: science, technology, engineering, and medicine) and its strategic development plan – 'China 2025'. This part aims to help readers assess the long-term *technological competence* of Chinese firms. The second part of the chapter looks at China's *trade relations* with other nations. An understanding of this macroenvironment offers the reader a foundation to understand the growth potential of Chinese firms. The final part of the chapter looks at China's *economic co-operation* with other nations. It pays special attention to China's BRI (Belt-and-Road Initiative), which covers over 120 countries and 40 per cent of the world's GDP (Shepard, 2016). Thus, the way this initiative unfolds will have significant impacts on Chinese firms. While these three domains do not exhaustively include all factors affecting Chinese firms, they highlight the boundaries within which Chinese firms operate and prosper in the global economy.

9.2   TURNING POINTS

9.2.1   *From Awareness to Catching Up with World's Tech Competence*

When China's former president Mr Deng Xiaoping led the nation's economic reform in 1978, he took a ride on Japan's high-speed rail for the first time. This experience made a deep impression on him as he became acutely aware of the technological gap between China and the developed world. He realised how important it was for China to catch up on the technological front. Otherwise, the nation's future would be bleak.

At the time Deng embarked on the Japanese train ride, it was just over a decade after China broke off its strategic alliance with the former Soviet Union, which lasted from 1956 to 1966. China was extremely weak in terms of its technological infrastructure, assets, and talents in 1978. Indeed, the country had been slipping behind as the developed world advanced on the technological front. Awakened to this reality, Deng realised the urgent need to catch up, so he posited technological advancement as the cornerstone of China's modernisations plan. He gave a mandate that all Chinese firms learn from their foreign joint venture partners. Up to the present day, the hunger for foreign technology has been a key motive in most Chinese joint ventures.

In the midst of this humbling experience, when Deng praised Japan's iconic bullet-train technology, no one would have forecasted that, forty years later, the situation would reverse. Today, China undisputedly outcompetes Japan in its high-speed rail transportation on a global scale. Similarly, in 1978, when less than 5 per cent of Chinese families owned televisions, refrigerators, washing machines, cars, and home phones, no one would have imagined that China would become the world's largest producer and user of these products.

From 1978 to 2008, China gained ground catching up with the rest of the developed world by mastering much of the needed technology in manufacturing. This was achieved through continuous learning from their joint venture partners coupled with occasional indigenous breakthroughs, thus earning the country's world-factory status. By 2015, China was producing about 80 per cent of the world's air conditioners and 70 per cent of the mobile phones. Together with supply chains that spread throughout Asia, China and its Asian partners make almost half of all the world's goods (Economist, 2015).

9.2.2   China's Tech Strength and STEM

The second wake-up call for China regarding the need to own and build its technological asset came at a surprise to most Chinese people. This happened when the USA encountered the financial crisis in 2007, during which, it blamed China for its job losses in manufacturing. It also attributed many of its problems to the rise of China (Grenville, 2013). In addition, the US government took an American-centric approach and adopted quantitative easing (increasing the money supply at a low to zero interest rate) to fix its financial crisis with little regard for other economies. For six years, the American-centric approach to recovery (2007–2013) left a relational scar with its trading partner nations.

As the US government worked diligently to recover from the crisis, China continued its economic advances and gained increased respect from the nations it worked with. As well, China gradually built up its R&D infrastructure and talent pools. With three decades of continuous growth in the manufacturing sector, China's robust economy emerged as a buzzing world market for firms from other nations. Most MNCs that entered China for its market from 2005 to 2012 received handsome rewards. Annual member surveys by various chambers of commerce (e.g., American Chambers of Commerce) during this period revealed that most firms regard China as a rewarding world market. These American firms made genuine demands for policy changes and agreed with what the Chinese government has done. Through strong local demands, open-market policy, and responsiveness in administration, China has continuously gained the trust of its trading partner nations and MNCs.

FIGURE 9.1 Number of STEM graduates across leading nations, 2016
Source: World Economic Forum (2016)

During this busy development period, China's technological talents and infrastructure gained momentum. The nation's growth in tech strength was more accidental than planned and thus was scattered. Nonetheless, Chinese firms, both private and state-owned, and booming universities formed a solid base to provide a consistent supply of STEM talents that totalled 4.7 million graduates per year (Figure 9.1). Accordingly, China's trusting relationship with its trading nations and its supply of technological talents enabled President Xi Jinping to draft his visionary plan for China when he assumed leadership in late 2012.

In an Organisation for Economic Co-operation and Development (OECD) study (2018) on the global distribution of tech talent among G20 nations, China is in the lead with 37 per cent, followed by India (26.7 per cent), Russia (4.5 per cent), the USA (4.2 per cent), and Indonesia (3.7 per cent). These leading tech countries are followed by other developed nations such as Japan (1.9 per cent), the UK (1.4 per cent), and Germany (1.4 per cent). A similar pattern can be seen in the number of PhD graduates. While both China and the USA have around 50,000 PhD graduates per year, 80 per cent of American graduates are foreigners (and a majority of them hold Chinese visas). Although some of the foreign American

PhD graduates may choose to work in the USA, China has a larger pool of PhD graduates than the USA and other nations.

In addition to tech talents, two additional factors are of interest: China's R&D expenditures (Figure 9.2) and its ability to generate technological patents (Figure 9.3). Before 2013, China did not pay much attention in R&D and invested less than 1.5 per cent of its GDP in R&D between 2000 and 2013. Chinese firms (whether state-owned or private) assumed a passive role, emphasising technology transfer instead of developing their own technology during this period. This tendency began to change in 2013, and, by 2016, China became the world's second spender in R&D, just behind the USA. The strong push for R&D also occurred at the firm level. Firms such as ZTE and Huawei were among the top ten corporate investors in R&D by 2015. The heavy investments resulted in a strong rise in the number of technological patents filed by Chinese firms.

Despite these impressive statistics, there are notable caveats in China's achievements. Among the three types of patents filed (basic, design, and applied), China falls behind in basic scientific patents. This suggests that China is weak in its technological foundation.

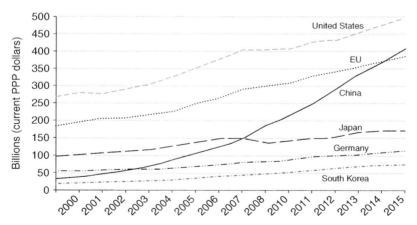

FIGURE 9.2 R&D expenditures of leading nations, 2000–15
Source: OECD (2016)

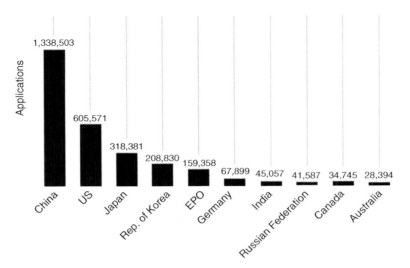

FIGURE 9.3 Patent applications of leading nations, 2013
Source: World Intellectual Property Organization (2017)

Further, a large proportion of new products made in China rely on patents licenced by non-Chinese firms. The lack of ultimate ownership in intellectual property rights may limit the future proliferation of new products from China. Third, without a solid scientific base, Chinese firms may not be able to achieve major breakthroughs. Today, both the government and firms recognise these weak spots and are eager to acquire original patents through M&As to contribute to future growth.

9.3 CHINA DREAM AND 'CHINA 2025'

When Xi Jinping assumed his leadership of China in November 2012, he drew upon China's trusting relationship with other nations, technological achievements, and supply of tech talents to formulate a developmental plan for the nation, the 'China Dream'. Unveiled in 2013, this blueprint for the nation lays out China's achievements, challenges, and future strategies. As a collective aspirational goal, it was also translated into ideals for individual Chinese people as

President Xi encouraged the young generation to 'dare to dream, work assiduously to fulfil the dreams and contribute to the revitalisation of the nation'. This ideal was subsequently popularised by government officials and journalists via official sites and public announcements.

Beyond the 'China Dream', the state council unfolded the 'China 2025' plan in 2015 with several purposes (China State Council, 2015). First, this plan is intended to help China overcome hurdles to growth such as the 'mid-income trap' (referring to the phenomenon where most advancing economies encounter socio-economic and political issues that derail them from further economic growth). Second, the plan is the executional core of the 'China Dream', as it enables the nation to reach its dream of being a great nation. Third, the 'China 2025' plan contains comprehensive guidelines regarding which industries will be the targets of development, the priorities for growth, and the support mechanisms that will ensure these industries' succeed. In short, the plan, when duly executed, will empower China to become a world leader in innovation.

The 'China 2025' plan was initiated by Premier Mr Li Keqiang and his cabinet. It borrows key insights from Germany's Industry 4.0, a cross-industry platform where a product's entire manufacturing process is optimised. Thus, following a customer's decision on a customised purchase (e.g., car), all the specifications of this purchase will then be aggregated and distributed to relevant firms to coordinate material sourcing, shipping, and logistics. The production will be tightly coordinated down to the finest detail to reduce material wastage and slack times known to plug the conventional supply chain, thus improving productivity.

Compared with German firms, Chinese firms are well behind in both production precision and IT coordination, let alone detailed multi-industry coordination. Accordingly, China is just moving from Industry 2.0 to Industry 3.0, with Industry 4.0 still being a significant distance away. Nonetheless, the idea of a highly coordinated, multi-industry strategic development is highly appealing to China.

Table 9.1 *'China 2025' at a glance*

Strategic sectors	
Advanced IT	Rail transport equipment
Aerospace and aeronautical	Maritime equipment and shipping
New-energy vehicles and equipment	Agricultural equipment
Automated machines and robotics	New materials
Biopharma and medical products	Power equipment

Strategic priorities	Support mechanisms
Manufacturing innovation capability	Institutional mechanism reform
Integration of it and industry	Fair market environment
Fundamental industrial capabilities	Financial support policies
Quality and branding	Fiscal and taxation policy
Green production	Multilevel talent cultivation systems
Breakthroughs in major areas	Small and medium enterprise policy
Manufacturing structural adjustment	Manufacturing openness
Service-oriented manufacturing	Organisation and implementation system
Manufacturing internationalisation	State Council oversight and support

Source: China State Council (2015)

China's State Council designed 'China 2025' as a multisector plan, with ten technological sectors (advanced IT, aerospace and aeronautical, agricultural equipment, robotics, biopharma and medical products, maritime and shipping, new energy vehicles, new materials, power equipment, and rail transportation). These sectors in turn have *nine priorities*, including innovation, IT integration, industrial capabilities, branding, 'green', break-through, structural adjustment in manufacturing, service, and internationalising manufacturing (see Table 9.1).

'China 2025' is a grand plan that builds on the nation's strength in its market (with China being the world's most populous), enterprises (both SOEs and the POEs), and talents (i.e., STEM). In addition to the ten selected sectors and their respective strategic priorities, the plan also identifies nine supporting mechanisms that need to be reformed to ensure that the goals for 'China 2025' can be achieved. One goal is to increase China's own supply of core materials to 40 per cent by 2020 (and 70 per cent by 2025) in its products. These mechanisms include institutional reform, financial market policies, tax policies, fair competition, talent cultivation, and governance. In sum, 'China 2025' is an ambitious plan, building on the nation's economic might and technological competence. It charts a growth path for China's tech competence with significant global influence.

9.4   SINO-AMERICAN TRADE RELATIONSHIP

By coincidence, 'China 2025' was proposed around the same time Mr Donald Trump won his presidency in the USA, who proposed 'to make America great again'. As China's future rise in economic strength is seen as a challenge to the USA, whose global leadership it has maintained since World War II, the visions of the two nations may clash as each competes for global leadership in economics, technological advances, and political influences. Mr Li Keqiang, China's premier, posited that 'China 2025' would be in line with the country's WTO obligations and the nation's right to develop. However, in 2018, the Council on Foreign Relations, a US policy think tank, stated that 'China 2025' would be a 'real existential threat to US technological leadership'. This perception was reinforced when they examined the blueprint of 'China 2025'.

On 15 June 2018, the Trump administration started a trade war between the two nations by imposing in stages tariffs on Chinese imports to the USA. The tariff covered a wide range of products included in 'China 2025', especially those in IT and robotics. Whereas the Trump administration argued that the purpose of the tariffs was to 'level the trade balance' and 'regain the manufacturing jobs that have been lost', the trade war was seen by others, including the Chinese government, as a way to derail, if not halt, China's technological development and its growing economic strength. Indeed, some observers have pointed out that the high unemployment rate in some US states, in particular the traditional manufacturing states, is caused by regional job disparity rather than trading with China (Bivens, 2018). In addition to the trade balance and lost manufacturing jobs, there are other issues embedded within the trade war. They include US concerns with Chinese firms' sabotage of intellectual property rights and stealing of technology secrets from trading partners. If substantiated, these violations can further complicate the trade disputes.

Trade imbalance is not new, and, if it is just an economic issue, finding a solution is relatively easy. In most cases, the two countries would first assess the trend and the size of the imbalance. Then, the two governments could resolve the imbalance by agreeing on a schedule in which the nation that enjoys positive balances would buy more from the trade deficit nation. This has been the foundational principle in the WTO. As shown in Figure 9.4, the trade imbalance can

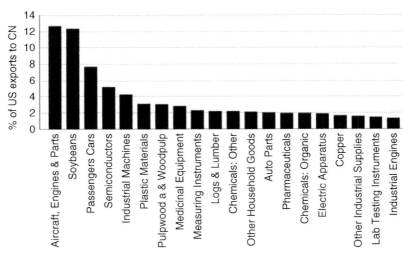

FIGURE 9.4 US–China trade by product categories, 2016
Source: International Trade Centre (2017)

be resolved if China agreed to purchase more of the top US exports to China (e.g., aircrafts, soybeans, cars, semiconductors, etc.).

On the other hand, when the trade balance is tied to other issues, it would be much harder to reach a solution. In the case of the 2018 trade dispute, the American tariffs on Chinese products apparently go beyond trade issues. With more tariffs on technological products than on food and consumer disposables, most observers believe that the Trump administration links the tariff issue with China's technological advancement (Lawder, 2018). In addition, the timing of the tariffs matched closely with the American midterm elections in November 2018, so it is likely that the tariff issue is also linked to US elections. In sum, there is a complex and interconnected relationship among three issues: trade imbalance, China's rise in technology advances, and American politics. As such, some observers are pessimistic that the Sino-American trade relationship can be resolved within a short time and lay to rest (Mayeda, 2018). The era of global competition between the USA and China may have begun.

The Sino-American trade war has strong repercussions for the world economy for several reasons. First, both nations are each other's top trading partner. Thus, any friction will severely affect the respective economies. Second, as the USA and China are the top two economies in the world, trade wars between them will likely slow the world's economic growth. Third, China has maintained a large and rising trade surplus with the USA, reaching USD375 billion in 2017 alone (Figure 9.5). This means that finding a solution will not be easy.

Given the severity of the issue, many organisations have offered their views and suggestions to help resolve the dispute between the two nations. Their insights may help chart a direction for a solution. For example, in the RAND *China and International Order Report*, Mazarr, Heath, and Cevallos (2018) found that, over the past two decades, China has not opposed or sabotaged the post-war international order, but rather it has behaved as a conditional supporter.

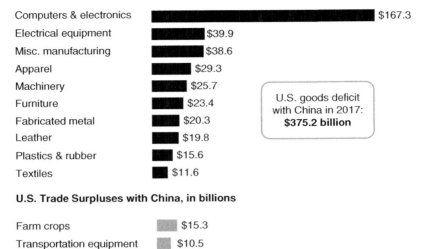

U.S. Trade Deficits with China, in billions

Computers & electronics	$167.3
Electrical equipment	$39.9
Misc. manufacturing	$38.6
Apparel	$29.3
Machinery	$25.7
Furniture	$23.4
Fabricated metal	$20.3
Leather	$19.8
Plastics & rubber	$15.6
Textiles	$11.6

U.S. goods deficit
with China in 2017:
$375.2 billion

U.S. Trade Surpluses with China, in billions

Farm crops	$15.3
Transportation equipment	$10.5
Oil and gas	$6.9
Waste and scrap	$5.5
Minerals and ores	$1.5
Forestry products	$1.1

FIGURE 9.5 US trade deficits and surpluses with China, 2017
Source: US Census (2018)

Thus, as China rises in economic strength, it may expect to exert more influence as a condition of its support on world issues. Second, the RAND report suggested that a strengthened and increasingly multilateral international order can function as a tool for the USA and other countries to shape the rising Chinese power. This is especially the case as China is still reforming its societal political institutions. Third, while China and Chinese-led initiatives do challenge US leadership and influence, they generally do not pose a threat to the fundamental integrity of the established international system. In conclusion, RAND points out that the growth of Chinese power is not something the USA can or should oppose; rather, the USA should develop a comprehensive strategy to sustain, expand, and monitor China's role in the international order.

9.5   CHINA'S BRI (BELT-AND-ROAD INITIATIVE)

Affected by complicated trade issues and spillover concerns, China is eager to partner with nations with growth potentials to continue to fuel its own economic growth. From China's perspective, other economies in Asia, Africa, and Europe are plausible partners. As discussed in Chapter 4, China's private firms find African nations especially appealing.

Interestingly, as China continues to seek new markets, the Beijing government has uncovered an appealing framework that may offer a long-term solution for its large manufacturing capacity. In 2013, President Xi Jinping unveiled the BRI during his visits to Kazakhstan and Indonesia. In many regards, the BRI is part of China's effort to leapfrog the nation into the new century. Later, the initiative was promoted and reinforced by Premier Li Keqiang during his visits to Asia and Europe. The BRI was intensively covered by the state media. By 2016, it became the most frequently mentioned concept in the *People's Daily*. The BRI has several key characteristics, as outlined in the following.

First and foremost, the initiative is the largest developmental plan in the history of the world economy. As Figure 9.6 shows, it is geographically structured along several land corridors and sea channels in the Asia-Pacific, Middle East, and Europe. It covers more than 120 countries, including 65 per cent of the world's population and 40 per cent of the global GDP as of 2017 (Table 9.2). Accordingly, it is the largest infrastructure and investment project in history. As a collection of economic, cultural, and technology systems and mechanisms, the BRI aims to construct a large economic land mass that encompasses domestic and international markets along its path. The BRI calls for mutual understanding and trust of member nations through cultural exchanges. It also has the potential to lead to new patterns of capital inflows, talent migration, and technological advances. Initially, the BRI focuses on infrastructure investment, education, construction materials, railway and highway, automobile,

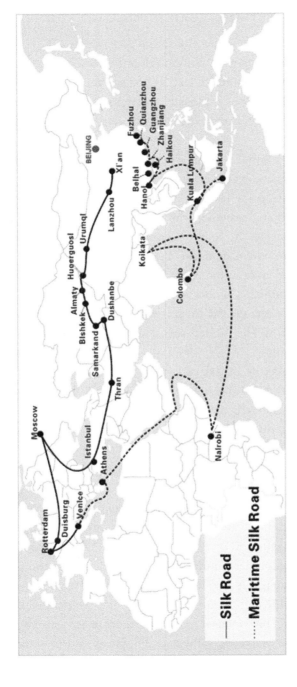

FIGURE 9.6 Map of China's BRI
Source: China State Council (2018)

Table 9.2 *Nations involved in China's BRI*

East Asia	West Asia	Mid-South Asia	Commonwealth of Independent States	Mid-East Europe	West Europe
Korea	Armenia	Afghanistan	Azerbaijan	Belarus	Austria
Mongolia	Azerbaijan	Bangladesh	Belarus	Bulgaria	Luxembourg
Thailand	Bahrain	Bhutan	Kazakhstan	Czech Republic	Switzerland
Laos	Georgia	India	Armenia	Hungary	Italy
Philippines	Iraq	Iran	Moldova	Poland	Portugal
Brunei	Israel	Pakistan	Russia	Romania	
Vietnam	Jordan	Sri Lanka	Tajikistan	Slovakia	
Cambodia	Kuwait	Maldives	Ukraine	Albania	
Myanmar	Lebanon	Nepal		Bosnia and	
Indonesia	Qatar	Uzbekistan		Herzegovina	
Malaysia	Saudi Arabia	Kyrgyzstan		Croatia	
Singapore	Palestine	Turkmenistan		Greece	
Timor-Leste	Oman			Slovenia	
	Turkey			Malta	
	United Arab			Montenegro	
	Emirates			Estonia	
	Yemen			Latvia	
	Syria			Serbia	
				Lithuania	

Source: Hong Kong Trade Development Council (2019)

real estate, power grid, and iron and steel to address the 'infrastructure gap' of the nations involved. When these needs are met, the BRI may then take up other activities to accelerate economic growth in the nations concerned.

Second, the BRI requires USD900 billion of infrastructure investments per year over the next decade. This can be accomplished through debt instruments, which would account for 50 per cent of the infrastructure spending rates. To finance the projects, China established the Asia Infrastructure Investment Bank in December 2015, with eighty-seven member nations. The bank started with USD100 billion capital, amounting to two-thirds of the capital of the Asian Development Bank and about half that of the World Bank. In addition, China has two additional funds to support the BRI. These are the Silk Road Fund (USD40 billion) and China's Export Bank Fund (USD50 billion).

Third, the BRI involves some neighbouring nations that have had historical conflicts (e.g., Pakistan and India, Russia and the Ukraine, etc.). This situation implies that regional co-operation may be difficult to obtain. In response, China has called for BRI nations to be rational in their approach in order to place their development needs over their conflicts with other nations. However, this assumption is bold and China does not have many options in the events that the BRI becomes entangled in disputes among nations. Indeed, disputes have already surfaced in a Pakistan BRI project that involves land claims by India.

Fourth, the BRI calls for long-term commitments signed by the government of the member nations. However, such agreements may not be fully honoured when governments change hands as a result of elections in the focal nations. This has already occurred in the case of the signed USD34 billion transportation and infrastructure project in Malaysia. In July 2018, the newly elected President Mahathir wanted to renegotiate the terms of the signed agreement because he estimated that the signed agreement would put Malaysia in a long-term debt position that the nation cannot afford. Similar concerns have been expressed by the newly elected prime minister of Pakistan, Mr Imran Khan (Jorgic, 2018). While recent modifications (e.g., reducing and/or partitioning the project in different phases) will ease some short-term concerns raised by the Malaysian and Pakistani governments, the long-term concerns remain to be resolved.

Interestingly, economists, sociologists, and political scientists have yet to properly conceptualise China's BRI in their theory frameworks to derive meaningful implications. Indeed, the concepts of "shared growth" and "common destiny" by BRI nations do not have a proper and agreed upon institutional framework (such as federalism). At present, most nations are using the incremental approach; that is, the member nations evaluate the benefits against the costs of joining (or not joining) the initiative. Seeing the growth potentials, so far most nations have chosen to join the initiative to avoid 'missing the boat'.

9.5.1 China's Persistence in the BRI

China is highly committed to the BRI despite the obvious challenges. There are at least three reasons underlying its commitment. First, the BRI reconnects China's past glamour to its present as a nation. The land that the Silk Road connected China to Europe via the mid-Asian nations was an icon in China's Tang Dynasty (AD 618–907), a period representing the high point in Chinese civilisation and a golden age of China's cosmopolitan culture. Its capital, Chang'an (present-day Xi'an) was the most populous city in the world at that time. The maritime Silk Road emerged some 400 years later in the Ming Dynasty (1368–1644), and the massive convoy of 240 ships established China as a peaceful empire that stretched from Northern to South-East Asia. Indeed, the land and the maritime Silk Roads were peaceful initiatives that benefitted all the nations involved. Framed in this positive and co-operative perspective, today's BRI serve two purposes. It aims to reduce other nations' doubts about partnering with China. Further, the plan rekindles the pride of the Chinese people to help achieve the collective ideal for the nation. This is why China's current leaders are committed to such an unprecedented plan.

Second, the BRI is timely. As China's production capacity (in infrastructure, transportation, telecommunication, and manufacturing) reaches a global high point, it thirsts for new markets. Without a consistent supply of new markets to unload China's productive capacity, China may lose its global manufacturing stature, thus leading to job losses. It will also be challenging for China to find sufficient jobs for its 7 million university graduates annually. More significantly, the many implementation challenges that the BRI will encounter (e.g., how the high-speed rail goes through jungles and plateaus) will present avenues through which China may enhance its tech frontier.

Third, the BRI is a platform that elevates China to be a global leader. Should this initiative be successful, China will be hailed as a moral and global leader with the integrity to help neglected economies to prosper. The African nations are good examples. Since World War II, Africa as a continent has been largely neglected by the world. Should only some BRI projects succeed, China may win credit in these projects. Even if all BRI projects fail, China may still be credited for its good intention. Accordingly, China may surely gain by proposing and coordinating the BRI.

Nonetheless, we hasten to point out that there is a worst-case scenario for China to pursue the BRI. Should the Chinese firms involved in these projects act selfishly and behave unethically, unprofessionally, and/or without caring for the benefits of the local consumers and employees, the good intention of the Chinese government will not hold and it would unfold the worst-case scenario for China.

9.6   IMPLICATIONS FOR CHINESE FIRMS GOING GLOBAL

After discussing the three domains that define the technological, commercial, and co-operative framework that the Chinese government have set up, the following paragraphs will explore how Chinese firms may use these institutional set-ups as they globalise their operations.

9.6.1 China's STEM graduates and other Tech Talents

The large pool of tech talents that China produces annually offers a competitive advantage to globalising Chinese firms. The consistent supply of STEM graduates allows firms to develop long-term expertise in selected industries of foci. This is critical in the future global competition in tech-related industries. As pointed out in previous chapters, Chinese firms are weaker than American and European firms in their management and branding talents. In this regard, the tech talents may compensate for, if not override, China's weaknesses in management and branding. So far, studies (e.g., Zhou, Yim and Tse 2005) have shown that Chinese talents have the capabilities to develop exploitative (vs explorative) innovations. That is, once they uncover the proper direction to innovate and possess the scientific patents to do so, the firms will flourish. However, there are two areas of concern.

First, foreign firms are also tapping into the Chinese talent pools. Since 2008, more than 500 MNCs have set up major R&D centres in China. Through these tech teams, many MNCs have developed highly successful products for the Chinese market as well as the market for other emerging economies. Thus, China's STEM pool is an open resource for firms from all nations. Chinese firms need to develop an innovative and technology-driven culture to benefit from this pool of STEM graduates.

Second, Chinese firms need to develop (or acquire the rights to use) scientific patents to develop new products. While Chinese firms score high on applied or design patents, they are weak in scientific patents as such patents typically require years of dedicated research work. Since 2008, the Chinese government has compensated this weakness by initiating various programmes to invite top scientists, especially those who own original patents, to work in China. Indeed, many scientists have contributed to Chinese firms through the 'thousand scientists' plan. Aside from government programmes, there are also corporate programmes (e.g., Cheung Kong scholar programme) that offer similar incentives. As well, Chinese firms have been actively acquiring firms with relevant scientific patents since 2015.

9.6.2   China's Trade Relations

The global proliferation of Chinese products implies that China's trade relationships with other nations are highly salient to Chinese firms. With strong competition in the home market, Chinese firms increasingly rely on foreign markets. Thus, the stronger China's trade relationship is with other nations, the better it is for Chinese firms to prosper. The recent trade dispute with the USA has hurt firms of both nations. While the dispute may have some silver linings for Chinese firms, most short-term effects are negative.

The potential fallout of the Sino-US trade dispute has caused the stock prices of many Chinese firms to drop to all-year lows while financial costs, such as loan interests, escalate. In particular, Chinese firms operating under the 'China 2025' initiative took a rollercoaster ride. When the initiative was announced, they were the foci of investors' interests and their positive future attracted attention in various stock exchanges (from Shanghai to New York and from Hong Kong to Singapore). However, as the Sino-US trade dispute gradually spilled over to the issue of global technology leadership, the future of these firms was perceived very differently by the investment community.

As investors had doubts over these firms' possible success, their stock prices fell. Many downgraded their future earnings. More importantly, these firms were increasingly monitored by foreign governments over potential tech and patent leakage. In some cases, their future expansion plans in host economies (e.g., the USA, Canada, the EU, and Australia) were scrutinised. In other cases, their planned acquisitions (of firms with patents) came to a halt as foreign (i.e., US) governments intervened (Fiegerman and Wattles, 2017).

Nevertheless, these seemingly negative events may have positive side effects for the firms concerned. First, the Chinese government may inject more financial support for these firms. After all,

'China 2025' is an aspirational plan embedded in China's future. Unless there is a major change in the government or its policy directions, it is inconceivable that this proposal will merely fade out. In this regard, firms in related industries will likely receive stronger government support because of the Sino-US trade dispute. This is especially true for the SOEs that will likely receive more government R&D funding and they may be granted more autonomy as a result.

Second, the Sino-US trade dispute will likely force Chinese firms to explore markets beyond the USA. Reducing Chinese firms' dependency on the US market may help them move towards a more diverse and sustainable model of development. Thus, while the trade dispute will bring short-term negative impacts on Chinese firms, be they private or state-owned, those that survive will receive long-term positive impacts given the push for market diversity and the injection of additional government support. In this regard, the BRI offers a timely opportunity.

9.6.3 BRI and the Sharing Model of Growth

China's BRI is a bold and unprecedented initiative that can be a game changer for not only Chinese firms, but also the world economy. This is in contrast to the American-centric approach of the Trump administration that has pushed many nations to search for opportunities in trade co-operation and economic development. However, for a megaproject like the BRI, it will take a long time before one can assess its result comprehensively. At the current time, the BRI has shown encouraging developments in Africa but its development in Malaysia and Pakistan has cast some shadows.

Nonetheless, if only a certain percentage of BRI projects can fulfil their goals, the positive impacts for Chinese firms will already be enormous. As many BRI projects are large in scale, they will generate consistent positive cashflow to the firms involved. Further, successful execution will likely elevate these firms to become global leaders in their respective industries, thus allowing them to be salient players in the world economy as American firms do now.

At the same time, products from China will have a solid beach-head in many countries along the land and maritime Silk Roads. These firms will take on a new and improved image. With new markets and an improved 'made-in-China' perception, the Chinese firms will have a highly favourable future in the BRI economies.

Another key benefit to Chinese firms is the opportunity to adapt their products to BRI countries. Rather than providing standardised solutions, Chinese firms that are marketing their products to the respective BRI countries will need to tailor their products to meet local needs. Whereas local demands may translate into higher costs and uncertainty for the firms, there are likely few competitors along the BRI and the project funding will be sufficient for the firms to cover the additional costs. In some ways, the BRI projects offer an assured path for product adaptation and exploitative innovation, thus enhancing the Chinese firms' ability to win future projects in the BRI countries.

Indeed, attracted by these growth potentials, privately owned Chinese firms are already requesting more support and opportunities to participate in BRI projects (Deloitte, 2018). In response, the Chinese government has written the BRI into China's constitution as of October 2017, assuring the participation of private firms.

It is important to note that the BRI complements 'China 2025' in two ways. Both initiatives involve firms of multiple industries; yet, 'China 2025' targets high-tech industries and their products need to break new technological ground. In contrast, the BRI is relevant for firms in traditional infrastructure, power-plant construction, telecom, transportation, and manufacturing industries. As a result, the two initiatives will not compete for the same groups of firms. Further, the two projects have different risk profiles. The BRI is challenging because it may involve nations that have historical disputes. The 'China 2025' initiative, however, can be interpreted as a direct challenge to the American global leadership. As a result, the risk is inevitable.

While the BRI is beneficial to Chinese firms, it is important to point out that it is a China-led but not a China-only initiative. In many cases, Chinese firms will need to compete with firms from other nations. Their chance to succeed will depend on how the Chinese government balances diverse firm interests. In sum, the ability for Chinese firms to compete fairly with firms from other nations as well as their ability to deliver the established goals are key to these firms' growing stature in the global economy. After all, the strong talent pool China has created, the trade relations China offers, and the two initiatives form a competitive arena but not a captive market for Chinese firms.

REFERENCES

Bivens, J. (2018). Recommendations for creating jobs and economic security in the U.S.: making sense of debates about full employment, public investment, and public job creation. *Economic Policy Institute*. 27 March. Retrieved 15 July 2019. https://epi.org/142207.

China State Council. (2015). 国务院关于印发《中国制造2025》的通知 [State Council's distribution of the 'made in China 2025' notice]. *China State Council*. Retrieved 15 July 2019. www.gov.cn/zhengce/content/2015-05/19/content_9784.htm.

China State Council. (2018). The belt and road initiative. China State Council. Retrieved 15 July 2019. http://english.gov.cn/beltAndRoad/.

Deloitte. (2018). Embracing the BRI ecosystem in 2018: navigating pitfalls and seizing opportunities. *Deloitte*. Retrieved 15 July 2019. www2.deloitte.com/cn/en/pages/soe/articles/embracing-the-bri-ecosystem-in-2018.html.

Economist. (2015). Made in China? *The Economist*. 12 March. Retrieved 15 July 2019. www.economist.com/leaders/2015/03/12/made-in-china.

Fiegerman, S. and Wattles, J. (2017). Trump stops China-backed takeover of U.S. chip maker. *CNN Business*. 14 September. 15 July 2019. https://money.cnn.com/2017/09/13/technology/business/trump-lattice-china/index.html.

Grenville, S. (2013). Blame China for the global financial crisis? *The Interpreter*. 23 September. Retrieved 15 July 2019. www.lowyinstitute.org/the-interpreter/blame-china-global-financial-crisis.

Hong Kong Trade Development Council. (2019). The Belt and Road Initiative: country profiles. *Hong Kong Trade Development Council*. Retrieved 15 July 2019. http://china-trade-research.hktdc.com/business-news/article/Th

e-Belt-and-Road-Initiative/The-Belt-and-Road-Initiative-Country-Profiles/obo
r/en/1/1X000000/1X0A36I0.htm.

International Trade Centre. (2017). International trade in goods – exports
2001–2016, electronic dataset. *International Trade Centre.* Retrieved
15 July 2019. www.intracen.org/itc/market-info-tools/statistics-export-
country-product/.

Jorgic, D. (2018). Fearing debt trap, Pakistan rethinks Chinese 'Silk Road' projects.
Reuters. 30 September. 15 July 2019. www.reuters.com/article/us-pakistan-
silkroad-railway-insight/fearing-debt-trap-pakistan-rethinks-chinese-silk-road
-projects-idUSKCN1MA028?il=0.

Lawder, D. (2018). Trump to unveil China tariff list this week, targeting tech goods.
Reuters. 2 April. Retrieved 15 July 2019. www.reuters.com/article/us-usa-trade-
china-technology/trump-to-unveil-china-tariff-list-this-week-targeting-tech-goods
-idUSKCN1H90C3.

Mayeda, A. (2018). American voters just sent a surprising message about the trade
war. *Bloomberg.* 8 November. Retrieved 15 July 2019. www.bloomberg.com/n
ews/articles/2018-11-07/u-s-midterm-voters-sent-china-a-surprising-trade-war
-message.

Mazarr, M. J., Heath, T. R., and Cevallos, A. S. (2018). *China and the International
Order.* Santa Monica, CA: RAND National Defence Research Institute.

OECD. (2016). OECD science, technology and R&D statistics: main science and
technology indicators, electronic dataset. *OECD.* Retrieved 15 July 2019. https://
data.oecd.org/rd/gross-domestic-spending-on-r-d.htm.

Shepard, W. (2016). China's one belt, one road plan covers more than half of the
population, 75 per cent of energy resources and 40 per cent of world's GDP. *South
China Morning Post.* 21 June. Retrieved 15 July 2019. www.scmp.com/business/
china-business/article/1978396/chinas-one-belt-one-road-plan-covers-more-half
-population-75.

US Census. (2018). International trade data, electronic dataset. *US Census Bureau.*
Retrieved 15 July 2019. www.census.gov/foreign-trade/index.html.

World Economic Forum. (2016). Human capital report 2016: learning through the
life-course. *World Economic Forum.* Retrieved 15 July 2019. http://reports
.weforum.org/human-capital-report-2016/learning-through-the-life-course/.

World Intellectual Property Organization. (2017). WIPO IP statistics data center,
electronic dataset. *World Intellectual Property Organization.* Retrieved
15 July 2019. www.wipo.int/edocs/pubdocs/en/wipo_pub_941_2017.pdf.

Zhou, K. Z., Yim, C. K., and Tse, D. K. (2005). The effects of strategic orientations
on technology- and market-based breakthrough innovations. *Journal of
Marketing,* 69: 42–60.

10 Holistic Conclusion through a Futuristic Lens

10.1 INTRODUCTION

From a humble beginning around twenty-five years ago, Chinese firms began their globalisation process and have since expanded to various industries in many parts of the world. As earlier chapters have shown, they have done so for two key reasons: to leverage their cost advantages in China and to transform their operations to become competitive in the global economy. Today, we are no longer witnessing only the global presence or the footprints of Chinese firms. Their representation in the Fortune Global 500 of 2018 (i.e., three of the top ten firms, eleven of the top fifty firms, and 120 of the top 500 firms) shows that their growth momentum is unprecedented in corporate history. Some Chinese firms are becoming global game changers.

This chapter is composed of three parts. The first part covers the four domains in which selected Chinese firms became game changers. It includes a discussion on the nature, types, and extent of changes these firms have brought about. The second part of the chapter points out the growing challenges faced by globalising Chinese firms. We posit that the global views on Chinese firms are fair and that how Chinese firms manage their operations and M&As in overseas markets will be salient in how they are perceived. In the third part of the chapter, we take a futuristic lens and propose how 'Chinese firms going global' will evolve. We discuss how the way in which the world accepts these globalising Chinese firms may have an impact on their growth paths and future.

10.1.1 Current State of Globalised Chinese Firms

Earlier chapters postulated that Chinese firms are making significant footprints in all corners of the global economy. Today, collectively, their stature has changed from being present to being salient, from leaving some footprints to becoming highly significant players. Indeed, some Chinese firms are becoming global game shakers in several domains.

As reported in the Fortune Global 500 in 2018 (Fortune, 2018), Chinese firms' size (measured by sales volume) and growth momentum were both salient and unprecedented in global corporate history, with State Grid (second), Sinopec (third), and National Petroleum (fourth) being among the world's top ten firms. In addition, China State Construction Engineering (twenty-third), Hon Hai Precision Industry (twenty-fourth), ICBC (Industrial and Commerce Bank, twenty-sixth), Ping An Insurance (twenty-ninth), China Construction Bank (thirty-first), Agricultural Bank of China (fortieth), China Life Insurance (forty-second), and Bank of China (forty-sixth) were among the world's largest fifty firms. In total, there were 120 Chinese firms on the top 500 list. When viewed as a group, Chinese firms are just behind US firms, of which they are only six more among the top 500.

As one would expect, SOEs are heavily represented among these 120 firms, including many in the banking, raw materials, and real-estate sectors. Most interestingly, private firms, and especially those in the high-tech sector (JD.com, Lenovo, Huawei, Baidu, Tencent, Alibaba, etc.), are also well represented.

Beyond their sheer size, Chinese firms are also making an impact globally. As they gain global stature, they are also becoming key players that can shake and reform the industries in which they operate. The following sections highlight four domains that Chinese firms have shaken up. These domains have been discussed in previous chapters, but summarising them here allows a holistic picture to emerge. The four domains are: (1) firm growth models, (2) industry leadership, (3) firm–government relationship, and (4) host–government relationship.

10.2   CHANGING MODELS OF GLOBALISATION

10.2.1   *Alternative Models of Globalisation*

A number of Chinese firms have pioneered new globalisation models. While conventional globalisation models advocate that a firm should globalise its operations to take advantage of its strengths and leverage them in overseas markets, most Chinese firms globalise in order to build their strengths. In the conventional view, these firms are non-competitive and have no capability to become global players. However, by going abroad, these Chinese firms are able to access richer talent pools, obtain cutting-edge technology, and learn to compete globally. In so doing, many of them have transformed into competitive global firms.

As Luo and Tung (2007) showed, these firms perceived the global business environment as a springboard that enabled them to learn and to perform at a level higher than they could have reached if they had remained in China. By going abroad, they elevated their technological, competitive, operational, and managerial competences. The springboard model has since evolved to include variants, such as the leapfrog model and the mixed model, that especially accommodate technological firms and SOEs, respectively. These models together refine conventional organisational logic and extend the 'world is flat' postulate to firms from emerging economies. While the 'world is flat' rationale has been used to benefit firms from developed economies to source low-cost production sites and sell the finished products globally, the success of Chinese firms via the springboard model shows that the 'flat' global environment can also function as a transformative platform for firms from emerging economies.

For SMEs that do not have the financial resources to adopt the springboard model, their expansion into global markets is made possible by the owners' entrepreneurial spirit and simple heuristics afforded by the effectual model. While SME owners are likely risk-takers, they need to be highly cautious in assessing the risks they take for their businesses to survive. This is especially important when they expand globally. Instead of laying out an optimal strategy and then looking for resources (e.g., bank loans) to execute the plan as big firms do, SME owners, who may have difficulties obtaining a bank loan or a governmental guarantee, need to size up the opportunity, assess whether they can afford the risk, and then act quickly to seize the opportunity. This effectual model, which relies on simple decision heuristics instead of detailed planning, offers the flexibility many entrepreneurial firms need to succeed in unknown territories, such as the African market, to seize the opportunities as they emerge.

10.2.2   *More about the Springboard Model (and Its Variants)*

Firm experiences show that the springboard model with its characteristics allows firms under certain conditions to succeed. First, these firms need to have (or be able to obtain) *sufficient financial resources* to acquire technology, talent, and other proprietary assets (brand names, channels) in the global environment. In general, financial capability is a top priority for firms that do not have the competitive advantages to go global. In China, however, SOEs enjoy amble financial support from the government and became the first group of Chinese firms to expand globally. As of February 2017, their debt-to-asset ratio reached 66 per cent (Xinhua, 2018).

Chinese firms that do not have the financial support enjoyed by SOEs can obtain financial support from the stock market to fuel their global expansion. After China set up its stock exchanges two decades ago, its stock exchanges (in particular, the stock exchange in Shenzhen, China's Silicon Valley) is a warm bed for entrepreneurs and growing firms, especially in the new economy. Its IT sector, for example, is more than twice the size of the IT sector of the Shanghai Stock Exchange. While most of the world's stock markets trade at low price-to-earnings (PE) levels (less than 20), the comparable PE level for

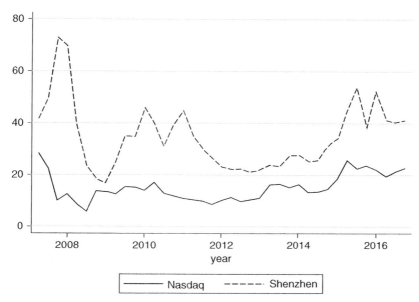

FIGURE 10.1 Comparison of PE ratios in Shenzhen and New York stock exchanges
Source: Nasdaq (2019)

stocks listed in Shenzhen is much higher at 40–60 (see Figure 10.1). With highly positive investor sentiments, POEs listed in Shenzhen (including many industrial products and high-tech firms) can obtain financial resources by being publicly listed on the stock market and using the springboard model to acquire other forms of competences globally.

Another qualifier for the springboard model is that the firms need to have a *large home market* to ensure that the globally acquired competences can be used to improve firm performance. Once again, China's SOEs are good candidates for this model. Given their dominance in some of the restricted markets in China, they can put their newly acquired competences to good use. These include state-owned banks and firms in strategic industries where the government chooses to exercise strong control. In these sectors, the SOEs have semi-monopolistic positions, such that the competences they acquire can be effectively and readily leveraged in the home market.

Some POEs in the home appliance (e.g., Haier, TLC) and Internet (e.g., Tencent, Alibaba) industries also have strong home markets. The large and fast-growing market in these sectors in China offers them important home advantages to allow them to leverage their globally gained competences. In 2017, China's real-estate firms performed well with strong market demands, and they are now becoming active globally. Driven by strong population growth and escalating prices in urban China, real-estate firms have emerged as the next group of firms adopting the springboard model to go abroad. The most noticeable example in this sector is Country Garden. In February 2017, it sold USD3 billion worth of properties in Malaysia. Other real-estate firms are also eagerly globalising their operations.

10.2.3   Other Models of Globalisation

Aside from the springboard model and the effectual model, would other globalisation models emerge from Chinese firms' experiences? We expect this can happen for two reasons. First, the major firm globalisation models (except for the springboard and effectual models) were developed more than three decades ago (see Table 10.1). However, considerable shifts in the economic landscape, advances in technology, changes in management thinking, and the exponential growth of the Internet have taken place over the ensuing period. Thus, it is just a matter of time before new models are likely to emerge to integrate and accommodate these changes.

Second, whereas Chinese firms have taken the lead in the development of new globalisation models, firms from India, Russia, and Latin American and Middle Eastern countries can also explore new ways to globalise and compete, given their respective cultural contexts and country advantages. We posit that selected firms from these economies will also assume unconventional ways to globalise and

Table 10.1 *Key firm globalisation models*

Globalisation models	Developed in	Key postulates
Comparative country advantage	1950s	Country leverages its cost advantages to export
Competitive firm advantage	1970s	Firm leverages cost advantages to export and FDI
Dunning eclectic paradigm	1980s	Firm leverages ownership, learning, and internationalisation advantages
MNC models (resource-based, JV, transactional costs, standardisation, network)	1980s	Firm leverages resource, partnership, standardisation, and network advantages
Springboard model and variants (leapfrog, mixed)	2007	Firm gains advantages globally
Effectual model	2012	Firm managed as entrepreneurial pursuit

succeed. Collectively, this will lead to the development of new models to enrich the study and practices of international business.

10.3 CHANGES WITHIN INDUSTRIES

Among the changes Chinese firms have brought about, the most significant changes have taken place in the industries in which they operate and, most noticeably, in their product offerings. As discussed in the case of Haier (Chapter 3), Chinese firms were able to maximise their cost advantages, produce products of a reasonable quality, and sell them at an affordable price. These products are highly sought after by consumers in developing economies as well as low-income consumers in developed economies. While established MNCs may consider these 'cheap' products to be of low profitability and not worth their efforts, Chinese firms are able to prosper as they manage to serve large groups of consumers by escalating their scale economy in production.

Accompanied by their successes, these 'cheap' products have since been relabelled as *'affordable innovation'* – that is, products of a reasonable quality offered at an affordable price to previously ignored consumers. This trend began in the 1990s with appliance manufacturers such as Haier, Hisense, and TCL that benefitted and grew by exporting affordable refrigerators, washing machines, and televisions globally at an unprecedented scale.

The trend of producing affordable innovation has continued as China gained its status as the world factory. Currently, personal computers, mobile phones, and other household appliances (air-conditioners, LED TVs, etc.) are flowing out of China continuously to reach the global market. In addition, machinery and equipment industries have also been affected by the affordable innovation trend from China (Tse and Wu, 2018). These inexpensive, made-in-China products are welcome in developing countries in Asia, the Middle East, and Africa. They also revive low-income markets in USA and Europe.

With China meeting the global demand in consumer and industrial products, these industries underwent a related change: a *shift in global supply chains.* This can be seen in neighbouring economies (Hong Kong and Chinese Taiwan), as well as countries further away (Korea, Japan, and the USA). As firms from these economies move their factories to China, manufacturing sectors in Korea, Chinese Taiwan, and the USA are hollowed out. Over time, as the supply chains in China become increasingly efficient, they drive the hollowing momentum to become faster and faster.

Over the last five years, labour costs in China have begun to rise sharply (CNBC, 2017). Accordingly, some firms are shifting their factories to lower-cost Asian countries. However, reorganising a firm's global supply chain takes time and planning. While some firms have started relocating their factories and supply chains, major changes have not yet taken place. The most serious challenge will likely come from India, given the country's strong supply of skilled labour, its large domestic market, and its maturing stock market. If these factors are triangulated well, India may repeat some if not all of China's growth pattern.

With the growing momentum and strong demand for their products, Chinese firms are also *reshuffling the firm ranks in various industries*. As Chinese firms become industry leaders, they gain leadership advantages in managing the value-chain and in making industry standard decisions. To put it simply, Chinese firms will increasingly set new industry standards in their favour to reinforce their future successes.

However, the change in industry leadership positions may come with potential negative effects, as many Chinese firms have not internalised the proper professional practices of established MNCs. In particular, the practices of delivering safe products and many best practices (such as being environmentally friendly, equitable employment, and behaving as a responsible stakeholder in host markets) have yet to be recognised by Chinese firms. Thus, leading Chinese firms have the potential to down-grade safety standards and firm best practices on a global scale. In addition, there are substantial gaps in how some Chinese firms manage their home and host country operations, with their operations in developing countries having a lower level of firm commitment in CSR practices. While we consider the contributions Chinese firms have brought to various industries, the dark side effects are potential risks of which industry practitioners need to be aware.

10.4 FIRM–HOME GOVERNMENT RELATIONSHIP

Another domain to which Chinese firms have brought changes is that of a firm's relationship with the home government. As mentioned, the SOEs are the first Chinese firms to globalise their operations, a move shaped and driven in part by their state-owned status. Unlike most developed countries, where government ownership often breeds organisational rigidity and mediocrity in firm performance, Chinese SOEs seem to perform well, outperforming their rivals in China and in the global economy.

Since 2012, the successes of Chinese SOEs have sparked interest among scholars and policymakers alike to re-examine the conventional argument against poorly performing government-owned firms. Some early studies showed that Chinese SOEs were inefficient organisations that lived off government protection as they monopolised markets, enjoyed low cost financial resources, and leveraged policy favours. Labelled as fiefs (Boisot and Child, 1996), these SOEs operated as corrupt organisations. They built capitalistic guanxi networks, twisted the free-market system, and derailed China's economic growth. In sum, China's SOEs were like little empires that helped some local governments become economic warlords (Walder, 1995).

These incidences cautioned the Chinese government to continuously reform the SOEs. While some SOEs were supported (e.g., China Petroleum, ICBC), many ailing SOEs were administratively reorganised or closed down (Lau, Tse, and Zhou, 2002). Meanwhile, selected SOEs were ordered to compete globally (Chalco and the Citic Group). In most cases, the SOEs installed stricter governance systems to reduce potential corruptive behaviours. The reforms proved to be effective, and the SOEs have gradually improved their capabilities over the last two decades. Major corruptive cases are getting fewer as the regulatory environment continued to advance.

The SOEs' contributions to China's growth are increasingly recognised by analysts, researchers, and policymakers. Recent studies re-examined the roles played by these firms and their contributions. As state-owned firms, their operations had to align with the needs of the country and were thus critical to China's employment stability, wage equality, technological development, and regional growth (Tse et al., 2017). Scholars reconceptualised this firm–government relationship as 'state capitalism'. Using an evidence-based approach, they adopted a more positive lens to assess China's SOEs and their contributions.

The positive impacts of China's SOEs, along with their growth and globalisation path, set in motion a holistic re-examination of the firm–government relationship in the policymaking domain. While policymakers in developed economies advocate privatising their government-owned firms, the success of China's SOEs has rekindled the idea that governments and SOEs may operate effectively and without corruption. In addition, the success of the SOEs has spurred interest among emerging economies, including India, Russia, Brazil, and Mexico, on how to engineer growth in their economies.

In the meantime, the private (publicly listed) firms in manufacturing (e.g., Haier), banking (e.g., China Merchant Bank), real-estate development (e.g., Country Garden), and high technology (e.g., Alibaba, Tencent, Xiaomi, and Huawei) are quickly expanding. Moreover, some entrepreneurial firms have ventured to establish operations in Africa. On the one hand, these private firms are leveraging their scale economy in the home market to gain strong footholds internationally, as the SOEs do. On the other hand, they benefit from the infrastructure provided by the government as they negotiate for R&D support and leverage the STEM pools that the Chinese government has built. The government's 'China 2025' initiative and BRI also provide directions for their ventures.

10.5   FIRM—HOST GOVERNMENT RELATIONSHIP

Another domain of change initiated by Chinese firms is that of their *relationship with host governments*. Without doubt, Chinese firms made a poor start in two ways. Some firms ignored safety standards and exported hazardous products that were widely publicised in the media and consumer blogs (Topping, 2007). Other firms were too zealous in their overseas operations and adopted overly aggressive actions in host markets, including cut-throat price wars in Spain, unethical labour practices in Africa, environmental hazards in Mid-Asian mines, and even corruption. These poor CSR practices were duly reported in the international media, affecting the firm and China's national image. In response, the Chinese government issued 'socially responsible practice' guidelines to Chinese firms operating overseas.

The unfavourable images of hazardous products and unethical practices also harm the firms' talent hires, success in project tenders, and even decisions in sensitive M&As. In the USA and Europe, the national image of China has fallen from 60 per cent to around 40 per cent and negatively affects Chinese firms' expansion in developed nations.

Lately, Chinese firms' image has begun to stabilise. Public opinions of China among Asian consumers were generally positive in 2015, led by consumers in Pakistan (82 per cent), Malaysia (78 per cent), Indonesia (63 per cent), and Korea (61 per cent). The positive perceptions are reflective of the economic benefits these countries receive from working with China. The perceptions towards China in Pakistan, the first country to receive China's BRI grants, is the most favourable at 82 per cent. The proposed initiative valued at USD46 billion (around 17 per cent of its GDP) provides an enormous boost to Pakistan's economy, with a proposed investment of USD12 billion in transportation and USD34 billion in energy (power plants).

In all regards, the BRI projects in which Chinese firms will be heavily involved are huge. They cover sixty-four countries and half of the world's population, 75 per cent of the world's energy resources, and 40 per cent of the world's GDP. Should the plan achieve even its most modest goals, the nations involved will likely form better impressions of Chinese firms, and firm–host government relationships may enter a new era (see Table 10.2). Instead of being perceived as firms with questionable integrity, their contributions may foster a co-evolving mindset that will further advance the globalisation of Chinese firms. While it is

Table 10.2 *Chinese firms' involvement in selected BRI transport infrastructure projects*

Country	Belgium	Greece	Djibouti	Kenya	Pakistan	Sri Lanka
Investment value (USD millions)	4	624	185	551	198	3,830
Investors	China Merchants	Cosco Pacific	Cosco China Pacific Merchants	China Road & Bridge	China paid for 80 per cent of the port's Phase I	China Exim Bank
				China Communications Construction Company		China Harbour Engineering
						China Communications Construction Company
						China Development Bank

Source: Lirios (2015)

uncertain whether China's proposed plan will reverse the down-ward trend of China's image, the stakes are high and have impli-cations far beyond economics.

10.6   CHALLENGES FACED BY CHINA'S GLOBALISING FIRMS

As Chinese firms are changing various domains in the global econ-omy, their behaviours also invite challenges. Earlier chapters have depicted some of these challenges, which continue to escalate. More significantly, the challenges are traceable to the increasing perception that China is becoming a global economic force.

During the first decade of Chinese firms going out (1990–2000), the world saw China as a developing country struggling to free itself from its entrenched social institutions. Following the fall of the for-mer Soviet Union, China was left alone by the global community to pursue its socialistic political ideology, as the general view posited China as a weak global player. On the economic front, however, China continued to expand its manufacturing base. By choosing to pursue labour-intensive industries with low technology and design values, the country was positioned at the bottom of the value chain. No one expected China to become a serious contender in the global economy. Accordingly, firms and nations alike have gladly supported China in its growing world factory status, and many of them have sourced from China. The concerns regarding Chinese firms were related to their unsafe products and pirated labels (Table 10.3).

During this period, the low end of the value chain suited China well. Although the profit margins were low, the world-factory status provided China with an important advantage: a reliable supply of jobs. Indeed, the combination of stable exports, low inflation, and close to full employment uplifted China's econ-omy into a robust growth phase. China reported an annual growth rate of 12 per cent in this first decade.

During the second decade, China's economic clout began to draw attention, especially after it joined the WTO in 2001.

Table 10.3 *Changing views on China and Chinese firms*

Globalisation of Chinese firms	The first decade (1990–2000)	The second decade (2000–10)	The third decade (2010–20)
China's economic clout	China is a developing economy	China is becoming a world economic power	China is becoming a game changer
China as an economy	China as world factory	China as world market	China as world player
Chinese firms	They are sweatshops producing standardised products	They are fast learners of average stature	They dominate using their size and purchasing power
Implications to global firms	Sourcing from China	Selling to China	Working with China
Global mindset on China	China needs to globalise	Few Chinese consumers are rich	China's mid-income consumers are growing
Key challenges faced by globalising Chinese firms			
Firm level	Unsafe products	Violations of intellectual property rights	Chinese firms' aggressive M&As
	Pirated brands and technology	Aggressive strategy and cut-throat pricing	CSR practices

Thereafter, with 8–9 per cent growth per year, China's economic growth expanded to several domains, including global export shares, FDIs, and global GDP share. Although the income disparity is high in China, the country has produced a sizable segment of rich entrepreneurs. Their surge in buying power was regionally concentrated, turning Shanghai and other major Chinese cities into hot consumer markets. Coincidentally, China's surge in consumption power coincided with the weakening of the consumer markets in North America and Europe. From 2008 onwards, China gained another label: the 'world market'. As a result, more than half of Fortune Global 500 firms entered China to pursue the consumer market.

During the second decade, China's entry into the WTO triggered yet another major change. Its firms (both POEs and SOEs) were competing with global firms. The Chinese firms proved to be fast learners and fierce competitors, turning China into a highly competitive marketplace. The WTO requirement also helped open regional markets that benefitted both local and foreign firms. Indeed, China became a bright spot in the global economy during that time.

The aforementioned events together affected the global perception of China. Shifting from an empathetic view that had welcomed China into the global economy during the past decade (1990–2000), global views were becoming increasingly sceptical towards China as a future economic power. The strong purchasing power of Chinese consumers, especially on luxurious products, together with the mega events China hosted (e.g., the 2008 Beijing Olympics), provided the foundation for a changing perception towards China. The image of China as a growing world power began to set in, and some 'China bashing' began to emerge. With mixed feelings, Chinese-made products were increasingly monitored by the global community, and any instances of failure were duly reported in the global community.

During the current decade (2010–20), Chinese firms and the Chinese government are increasing their global engagement. Chinese firms are becoming movers and shakers of the respective industries in which they operate. The global views on China have become more diverse. While the USA and EU perceptions of China continued to be somewhat negative, the views from Asian countries are more balanced, and the views from African countries are largely positive. This diversity of views has affected Chinese firms, with some of their aggressive M&A plans heavily scrutinised if not stalled or halted.

In response, the Chinese government has set up several strategic initiatives to help propel its firms into the global economy. As shown in Chapter 9, the Chinese government is building a pool of technology talent in an unprecedented scale. In 2016, the number of STEM graduates and PhD students trained in China outpaced the USA and other nations by a wide margin. In addition, the country has put forth the 'made in China 2025' initiative and the BRI, both of which are potential game changers in the global economy.

10.7 A NEW GLOBAL ECONOMY OR ANOTHER CORPORATE GRAVEYARD

How Chinese firms globalise in the world economy is an interesting yet complex topic. There are two extreme positions: (1) the globalising Chinese firms will offer sweeping changes that contribute to the global economy; or (2) the globalising Chinese firms will end up like once-powerful firms such as Sharp and Kodak that have since faded and lost their former glamour.

On the positive side, the momentum of Chinese firms and their strong learning culture suggest that their global move will continue and gather strength. China's past three leadership successions has been smooth. Thus, in the near future, these firms will have the advantage of a home market in a stable political environment that supports Chinese firms in their global endeavours. Among Chinese firms, SOEs will likely continue to receive strong government support as they grow and mature. In the meantime, the private/publicly listed firms can benefit from the country's continuous reforms of the stock market to finance their global expansion plans.

Beginning in 2000, Chinese firms have adopted the springboard model (or its variants) to invest in and operate in overseas markets. In so doing, they have enhanced their capabilities and, as discussed, changed the industries in which they operate. Through M&As and other means of growth, many Chinese firms will likely lead in their industries. Affordable innovation will continue to help improve living standards on a global scale, allowing consumers from developing nations to benefit from the globalising economy in which Chinese firms participate.

We posit that there are several limiting factors in the globalisation of Chinese firms. The first factor comes from within the firms. To date, the leadership and management capabilities of Chinese firms do not match their global stature. In addition, to highly distinguished entrepreneurs such as Zhang Ruimin (of Haier), Jack Ma (of Alibaba), Pony Ma (of Tencent), and Lei Jun (of Xiaomi), Chinese firms need a continuous supply of senior management talents that can oversee a firm's operations in multi-country corporate networks. China's top business schools, such as those in Peking University, Tsinghua University, Fudan University, and Jiao Tong University, have not yet offered related programmes to fill this need. While firms may outsource management talents from other global firms and from other countries, these senior executives unfortunately have their share of challenges. Thus, the lack of senior management leaders will be a limiting factor for the globalisation of Chinese firms.

Another factor that may affect the future of Chinese firms is the outcome of the BRI, which involves the Chinese government as well as many SOEs and POEs. Should this initiative be successful, the Chinese firms will become major winners and global leaders in their respective industries. On the other hand, should the BRI fail, the firms involved may suffer disastrous consequences. Further, failure of the BRI may spill over to other areas (e.g., capital crunch), causing damage to other Chinese firms and the BRI economy.

The success of BRI is highly uncertain for several reasons. This initiative is large in scale, requiring the host-country governments to be highly committed over a long period of time. Political uncertainty regarding the host governments may stall the megaprojects and derail their completion. This is especially the case for host countries that are politically relatively unstable. Further, the developmental needs of the BRI host countries are diverse, and it is challenging to come up with a plan that all partners can agree upon. Indeed, the challenges may go beyond financial matters. The ability of the Chinese government and host-country governments to navigate these challenges is at best doubtful. At present, China has not yet formulated a sustainable co-development plan in its Xinjiang province. The difficulty in finding a workable solution exemplifies the complexity and uncertainty of the BRI.

The third factor relates to the cultural sensitivity that Chinese firms need to show their host economies. It is imperative that the globalising Chinese firms embrace socially responsible practices. When the firms' contributions to the local community are vividly seen, the efforts will help mitigate the inevitable local resistance. In addition, the BRI is a multi-national endeavour. How the Chinese government treats firms from other nations in winning the projects will also be crucial to its success.

Will firms from other countries compete with Chinese firms in their global expansion? In the near future (e.g., the next five years), the chance of formidable competition is not high. Beyond that time frame, competition from Russian and Indian firms will likely emerge, although powerful competition is not likely. Instead, existing global firms will likely co-operate and compete (i.e., co-opetition) with the Chinese firms simultaneously in the global arena. These global firms will likely posit themselves higher in the value chain, with premium brand names and innovative products.

Notwithstanding these challenges, the future of globalising Chinese firms remains far from certain. There are two additional factors need to be considered. The first factor concerns these firms' image. Unfortunately, Chinese firms do not enjoy a positive image in the global community. To reverse the negative perceptions, Chinese firms need to showcase clearly their corporate citizenship and contributions to the global economy. Doing so would include improvements in the perceptions of their core operational practices (including product safety), management style (being open and transparent), and the ways they manage public sentiments (complaints and CSR practices) that together contribute to the holistic perceptions of the specific firms as well as Chinese firms in general. The second factor concerns uncertainty in regional (i.e., Asia and Middle East) political dynamics that are beyond the scope of this book and the authors' expertise. While economics can be a contributing factor, other factors such as cultural and nationalist sentiments may override the effects in the economic domain.

Amid these uncertainties, there is one confident projection. The success of Chinese firms has and will continue to stimulate firms in other emerging economies to go global. While the environmental conditions that gave rise to the success of Chinese firms are unique (a world that welcomed China's growth and an abundant supply of talent limited by the country's institutional hurdles) and might not be repeated, the unprecedented success of Chinese firms is nonetheless highly stimulating for entrepreneurs and policymakers.

10.8   CONCLUSION

This chapter provides an integrated view on the collective impacts of globalising Chinese firms and their contributions. It identifies and discusses four domains that Chinese firms have changed. In many regards, Chinese firms have overturned several accepted norms with regard to firm successes and globalisation. More importantly, the success of China's SOEs provides an innovative view on how firms and governments can work together. Their successes also have implications for host governments. In sum, while the globalisation of Chinese firms may be accidental, its implications are highly influential and revealing.

The chapter also highlights the challenges Chinese firms have faced over the past three decades. Some of the challenges are external, reflective of how the world has modified its perception as China gathers economic strength. As discussed, the world's perception is highly salient to Chinese firms and is intricately linked to their future. Based on past events, it is likely that the global perception has been fair and reflective of the sometimes unprofessional ways in which Chinese firms have conducted their global operations.

While most indicators point to the continuous growth of Chinese firms in the global economy, the chapter also highlights the underlying challenges and uncertainties that may affect their growth. In addition to the external factors outlined earlier, most of the challenges come from within. Thus, the future of Chinese firms are in their hands. Should they continue to improve and engage in practices that align with global expectations, their continuous success will be assured.

The authors would like to end the discussion with three remarks. First, judging from China's actions over the past two decades, the country did not oppose or sabotage the post-war international order, but rather behaved as a responsible and conditional supporter. Second, a strengthened and increasingly multilateral international order may function as a tool for the global community to co-evolve with the rising China. Third, the growth of Chinese economy is something that the USA (and the world) can accommodate and benefit from.

REFERENCES

Boisot, M. and Child, J. (1996). From fiefs to clans and network capitalism: explaining China's emerging economic order. *Administrative Science Quarterly*, 41(4): 600–28.

CNBC. (2017). 'Made in China' isn't so cheap anymore, and that could spell headache for Beijing. *CNBC*. 27 February. Retrieved 1 October 2018. www.cnbc.com/2017/02/27/chinese-wages-rise-made-in-china-isnt-so-cheap-anymore.html.

Fortune. (2018). Fortune Global 500. Retrieved 16 July 2019. http://fortune.com/global500/list/.

Lau, C. M., Tse, D. K., and Zhou, N. (2002). Institutional forces and organizational culture in China: effects on change schemas, firm commitment and job satisfaction. *Journal of International Business Studies*, 33(3): 533–50.

Lirios, D. (2015). New Silk Road trade to top US$2.5 trillion, says Xi Jinping. *China Topix*. 30 March. Retrieved 10 January 2019. www.chinatopix.com/articles/44159/20150330/new-silk-road-trade-to-top-2-5-trillion-says-xi-jinping.htm.

Luo, Y. and Tung, R. L. (2007). International expansion of emerging market enterprises: a springboard perspective. *Journal of International Business Studies*, 38(4): 481–98.

Nasdaq. (2019). Nasdaq PE ratio 2006–2018, electronic dataset. *Macrotrends*. Retrieved 16 July 2019. www.macrotrends.net/stocks/charts/NDAQ/nasdaq/pe-ratio.

Topping, A. (2007). Mattel recalls 1.9m potentially dangerous Chinese-made toys. *The Guardian*. 15 August. Retrieved 10 January 2019. www.theguardian.com/business/2007/aug/15/usnews.china1.

Tse, A. and Wu, J. (2018). Why 'Made in China 2025' triggered the wrath of President Trump. *South China Morning Post*. 11 September. Retrieved 10 January 2019. https://multimedia.scmp.com/news/china/article/made-in-China-2025/index.html.

Tse, C. H., Yu, L., Leung, F. F., and Tse, D. K. (2017). Understanding China's state capitalism through its SOEs: the effects of globalization and state ownership in the pursuit of economic and social goals. Working Paper, Contemporary Marketing Center, the University of Hong Kong.

Walder, A. G. (1995). Local governments as industrial firms: an organizational analysis of China's transitional economy. *American Journal of Sociology*, 101 (2): 263–301.

Xinhua. (2018). China's central SOEs see decline in debt-asset ratio in H1. *Xinhua*. 12 January. Retrieved 10 January 2019. www.xinhuanet.com/english/2018-07/12/c_137319969.htm.

Index

Haier in, 39
image of China in, 104, 161–4, 204
springboard model in, 198
Xiaomi in, 116
Malaysia Mining Co., 48
Managers as target audience, 8–9
Market acceptance of Chinese products
generally, 6
cultural openness and, 113–14, 118
evidence-based perception, changes in,
111–12
group-based perception, changes in,
114–15
individual perception, changes in, 113–14
new products and, 115–18
world-mindedness and, 114–15, 118
Marketisation of Chinese economy, 1, 16
Marriott International, 118
Mattel, 90, 105
Maytag Corp., 40, 41, 42
Ma Yun, 161
McDonald's, 97–8
McKinsey Global Institute, 72, 75–6, 157
Meneghetti, 40
Mengnui Dairy, 90
Mercator Institute, 98
Mergers and acquisitions (M&A)
generally, 24
by Chalco, 46–7
failures by globalising Chinese firms in
generally, 100
doubts regarding acquisition
motives, 97–9
long-term competitiveness, concerns
regarding, 98–9
national security concerns, 96–7
by Haier, 37–9, 40
by Huawei, 67–8
by Lenovo, 58–9
Mexico
corporate social responsibility (CSR) and
MNCs in, 136
globalisation in, 4
Midea Group, 98–9
Milk, product safety problems, 87–90
Millennium Development Goals, 125
Miller, Doug, 149
Ming Dynasty, 185
Mining industry, failures by globalising
Chinese firms in

negotiation, 93, 100
workforce management, 92–3
Ministry of Commerce, 158
Mistakes by globalising Chinese firms
generally, 87
exports and, 87–90
product safety and, 87–90,
99
sustainable market presence, inability to
gain, 91
Mixed model
generally, 5–6, 53, 79
SOEs and, 70–1
MNCs. *See* Multinational corporations
(MNCs)
Mombasa-Nairobi Standard Gauge Railway
(SGR), 137
Multinational corporations (MNCs)
corporate social responsibility (CSR) and
generally, 135
in Africa, 135–7
in developed economies, 137–9,
142
in emerging economies, 135–7, 142
development in China, 23
Dunning's OLI model and, 34–5, 42
globalisation and, 4–5
as international business players, 33–4
internationalisation advantages, 34, 42
locational advantages, 34, 42
non-ownership advantages, 53–4
ownership advantages, 34, 42
special economic zones and, 1–2
Myanmar, Chinese infrastructure
development firms in, 95

Nasdaq, 64
National developmental need model
generally, 5–6, 43–5
alignment with national plans and, 49–50
applicability to other firms, 49–50
Chalco and, 6
Dunning's OLI model versus, 43–5
learning capabilities and, 50
management capabilities and, 50
oil and gas and, 45
National image of China
generally, 7, 146–8, 165–6
advantages of positive image, 146–7
advertising campaigns to enhance